Offiah
My Autobiography

Offiah

My Autobiography

MARTIN OFFIAH
with David Lawrenson

CollinsWillow

An Imprint of HarperCollinsPublishers

To my parents, George and Regina Offiah, my brother Chike and sister Nina who have supported me throughout my career, and to Doug Laughton, who made it all possible

First published in 1997
by CollinsWillow
an imprint of HarperCollins*Publishers*
London

© Martin Offiah 1997

1 3 5 7 9 8 6 4 2

A CIP catalogue record for this book is
available from the British Library

ISBN 0 00 218778 7

Photographs supplied by Allsport, Mike Brett and Andrew Varley

Printed in Great Britain by Caledonian International Book
Manufacturing Ltd, Glasgow

Contents

Foreword
by Colin Welland

It must haunt him. If it doesn't, it should. A dozen years ago when I enthused over a certain Martin Offiah, a fleet-footed teenager wasting his time on Rosslyn Park's wing, a certain manager of Fulham Rugby League Club didn't want to know. Inevitably the word got out and the flying winger went to Widnes. And, as they say, the rest is history.

Wingers are the brilliance of Rugby League encapsulated. Some talk of pivoting stand-offs, kicking acting-halves, driving props, majestic centres and such great men as these ... but those that constantly flit through the memory, shining and indelible, are the darting, dancing stars whose beat patrols the touchline and whose brief is to thrill the crowd.

Brian Bevan, Tom Van Vollenhoven, Lionel Cooper, Billy Boston still devastate behind closed eyes such was their magic, their breathtaking speed and, most memorable of all, their keen sense of theatre. They knew they were good, enjoyed being special, rejoiced in delighting us all. To those names we may now add that of Martin Offiah.

Clem Thomas, the late great Welsh Rugby Union captain, once asked me to name the contemporary player, in both codes, whom I would best like to have on my team. Offiah was my choice and on seeing him at the height of his powers Clem agreed. He readily recognised not only the sheer pace of the man, but his imagination, his coltish flamboyance; yet it was his devastating unpredictability that Clem most enjoyed. 'They're hell to play against,' he said. There must be many who faced Offiah who would say 'Amen' to that.

I've seen him score some unforgettable tries, as we all have. But it was one which he *didn't* score which will lodge the lad in my memory bank forever. The first minute of the Lions tour of Australia in 1992, Sydney Stadium saw a break round the blind side deep in the British half and Offiah was dispatched on his way with all Australia gasping. Andrew Ettingshausen's despairing ankle tap denied us the crowning moment but recalling the shudder which rippled through that hard nosed Aussie crowd still sends a shiver of satisfaction down my spine. When he finally puts his winged feet up, Martin will join my beloved Brian Bevan as a man who thrills simply in the memory. Until then, may he long continue to thrill us for real.

1
The End of the Beginning

At midnight on 31 December 1995, I probably made some New Year's resolutions as the chimes rang out. To be honest, I can't remember what they were. But I'm sure they didn't include leaving Wigan, joining the London Broncos and returning to Rugby Union with Bedford.

I had a lot to look forward to that New Year's Eve. Wigan were to play St Helens in the final of the Regal Trophy; we were in line to be crowned as First Division champions for the seventh consecutive time; and the Challenge Cup was starting in January – and Wigan hadn't been beaten in the Cup for around 40 games, over eight years. And, apart from the Cup games, there'd be a break from rugby for a few months, because the new Super League was going to kick off at the end of March. Summer rugby was on the way, with firm grounds and the sun on my back – ideal conditions for my type of game.

Maybe it's just hindsight, but I don't remember being as excited at the prospects for the year ahead as I should have been. Perhaps it was because I'd achieved everything that I possibly could in Rugby League, and I was beginning to feel that I needed a fresh challenge. A Great Britain tour to Fiji,

Papua New Guinea and New Zealand was coming up in the autumn, but it seemed something of a low-key affair and I couldn't really get too excited about it – been there, done that, there was a certain sense of déjà vu about the whole thing. After all, I'd been on three Great Britain tours: to Papua New Guinea, Australia and New Zealand, in 1988; to New Zealand, in 1990; and to Papua New Guinea, Australia and New Zealand again, in 1992. Anyway, I felt that the tour would be a good opportunity for Phil Larder, the Great Britain coach, to blood some of the younger players – and I was sure he wouldn't mind me missing the trip. On the other hand, if the tour had taken in Australia I might have had second thoughts about not going.

Then there was Wigan. I couldn't imagine not running out onto Central Park in that cherry and white number five jersey, but in a strange way maybe we were just too used to winning. So much so that one of our main motivations, as far as Cup rugby was concerned, was almost fear – none of us wanted to be part of a team that lost the Club's fantastic cup record. But, at the same time, we knew that our run couldn't go on for ever. And it takes some of the joy out of victory if you know that everyone assumes you'll win, and there'll be banner headlines if you ever lose.

But, as I say, that may all be hindsight. Certainly the year started well enough for Wigan, and for me. We beat St Helens in the Regal Trophy final, at Huddersfield, and we clinched the First Division championship again by the end of January: it was a good way to round off the last Centenary Championship before Super League started. We beat Bramley in round four of the Cup, and there were two weeks before our fifth round tie against Salford. Graeme West, our coach, decided to give the lads a week off, and some of them went to Tenerife – not me, though, because I had some other commitments. Just as well, in fact, because their flight back was delayed by bad weather, and the team didn't get together until the Wednesday before the game, which was to be played on Sunday – normally we'd have a whole week to prepare for a game like this. I remember thinking that it just wasn't enough.

I'll tell you about the game later, but the fact of the matter was that Salford just outplayed us. There'd been many times during Wigan's fantastic cup run – 44 games, by now – that we'd come close to losing, but we'd always managed to pull through. This time we had our chances, but we simply couldn't get the better of them. And that was that. The run was over, and it didn't feel at all good to be part of the team that lost the record. Everyone in the dressing room was shell-shocked.

We had to be positive and pull ourselves together, though, because there was still the Super League title to aim for. We won our opening game, against Oldham, but then we had to take on St Helens, at Knowsley Road. As usual, it was an intense affair, stoked by local rivalries and played in front of a large crowd. We started well, but it wasn't my day, because someone landed on my back when I was tackled, mid-way through the first half, and I had to be helped off the pitch. By the end of the afternoon, the doctors had told me that I'd cracked a vertebra in my back and I'd be out for several weeks, and St Helens had come storming back at us to win the game.

As you'd expect, the newspapers jumped on the fact that we had lost two big games, and printed stories full of gloom and doom, saying that Wigan was on the wane. But the players were keen to prove them wrong over the rest of the season. And we were looking forward to the two cross-code challenge matches against Rugby Union champions Bath, in May, and to the Middlesex Sevens, because we wanted to show that we were more professional than the Union players, and more skilful than them, too. So we worked hard at some special training sessions designed to familiarise ourselves with Union laws and techniques. It paid off, because we hammered Bath under League laws, in my first game back after my injury, and I scored six tries.

Ten days later we played in the Middlesex Sevens, at Twickenham, and won the competition. This was a great thrill for me, because I'd played in the competition twice in my Union days and never managed to win; it was good to see some of my old friends from Union at the ground, too. Then came the return match with Bath, under Union laws. Quite a few people thought that we'd have a chance of beating them, but we didn't think that was very likely. Still, we gave it our best shot, and managed to score a couple of good tries – and we had two more disallowed. Even so, I think that we made one or two people sit up and take notice of the league players' skills. And the League supporters began to realise that playing Union wasn't as easy as it looked. As far as I was concerned, I was impressed with the way the Union game had developed since I'd left it, and I liked the idea that the game had become professional – in name at least, though not yet in attitude, perhaps.

For me, though, it was back to the Super League, as well as a game for England against France, at Gateshead, on 21 June. As far as I was concerned, life was back to normal. You can only work out the way a story has unfolded later, I know, but over the next few weeks a series of developments – I hardly knew about them at the time, let alone had the chance to control them – were to bring about major changes in my life. The only influence I had on the outcome was the way I reacted to what was happening.

I'd just scored a try for England against France when someone pushed me in the back and I stubbed my toe in the ground. I didn't think anything of it at the time, but I didn't play in Wigan's next match, against Oldham. On 21 June I was in the side to play St Helens. They headed the Super League table, but we were only three points behind them, and we wanted to prove a point by taking revenge for what had happened earlier in the season – that game had been our only Super League defeat. And we did it, winning 35–19 with a great performance. We were only one point behind them, with half the season to go and everything to play for. But not for me. That was my last game for Wigan.

My toe was still troubling me, and I was out of the side while I had treatment to try to sort the problem out. And that gave me the opportunity to think about things – when you're playing you just don't have the time to sit down and work out what you want from your life. The fact is that I was becoming restless.

On one level, I felt I'd achieved everything that I possibly could in Rugby League and needed a fresh challenge; it was rather similar to the feeling when I decided to leave Widnes, in 1991. But where could I go? I still had a three-year contract with Wigan, and I didn't really want to leave the club that I considered the best club in the world. I really couldn't see myself playing for anyone else.

Then there was the way I'd changed as a person. It had all started when I had a long talk with Shaun Edwards in a club in Stoke, at the end of the 1993/94 season. He said that I shouldn't spend all my time worrying about my performance, and I shouldn't expect to score a try or put someone else through every time I got the ball: all I could do was to give it my best shot. From that time on, I realised that rugby wasn't the be-all and end-all, and that there was more to life. And I started to come out of my shell during the 1995 season – in a strange way, it was rather as if I'd been reborn.

I also had to think about the financial side of things. It seemed to me that the only players who did well after leaving Wigan tended to be the ones who had left on their own terms: if you waited until the end of your contract, and it wasn't renewed, you ended up wondering what you were going to do. I remember Ellery Hanley telling me a long time ago: 'There's going to be a day when your time in the sun is over. You have to be prepared for that day and make sure that you've got everything out of the game that you possibly can financially, so when it does come you can say, "It's been a good crack, I've made a few bob out of it and I've got some great memories."

But I still didn't really want to leave Wigan.

Then I started thinking about Rugby Union, and realised that it might give me a way around the problem. I'd enjoyed the cross-code games, and they had opened my eyes to the way the game had changed. And not just on the field, because since the International Rugby Football Board, Union's governing body, had decided to allow professionalism, in August 1995, I could earn my living at the game – the fact that I hadn't been able to before was the reason why I had accepted Widnes' offer in the first place. The more I thought about it, the better the idea seemed to be. With Super League being played in the summer, there wouldn't be too much of an overlap with Union in the winter. I could have the best of both worlds. Anyway, the barriers between the two codes, which had existed for a century, had finally come down and Union clubs were looking to sign League players, following Wigan's success in the cross-code games and the Middlesex Sevens. I could try for a full England cap at Union, too – the furthest I'd got before was an England Students cap. But, above all, I'd have a new challenge.

So I asked Alan McColm, my agent, to try to get me a short-term contract that would allow me to play Union in the winter, between the end of the first Super League season and the start of the next one, in March 1997. Then a problem came up. Wigan said that they wouldn't allow any of their players to take up short term-contracts to play Rugby Union, because of the risk of injury and because they didn't want them to play rugby all year round, without a break.

But then another piece of the jigsaw slotted into place. What I hadn't known was that the club was financially stretched. I didn't know anything about the ins and out of Wigan's finances – like the other players, I wasn't aware of any problems because we all got paid on time. But, later, Jack Robinson, Chairman of Wigan, was to tell me that the first season of Super League had not gone well: crowds had been down; and the fact that Wigan hadn't reached the Challenge Cup Final at Wembley represented a huge loss of revenue for the club – there was nothing to worry about, he told me, but he made it plain that things were pretty tight. So Wigan changed their minds. They realised that allowing some of their players to take up short term contracts would mean the burden of paying players' wages during the winter would be passed to the Union clubs. Essentially, Wigan would be hiring players out for the off-season.

So now I had the green light. At first, I wanted to sign up with an English First Division club. There was some talk of me going to Bath, who ended up signing Wigan team-mates Henry Paul and Jason Robinson, and also of Newcastle – although they are Second Division side, they had the backing of Sir John Hall, who had poured millions into Newcastle United and had taken on Rob Andrew, the former England fly half, as Director of Rugby and recruited some top players. But I felt that I should be based near London, because I wanted to pursue other aspects of my career. I'd done some television work, appearing on various shows and acting in episodes of *Emmerdale* and *Hollyoaks,* and been given the opportunity to do more media work in London, but had to turn it down because I couldn't fit the travelling that would have been involved into my schedule.

None of London's big clubs were prepared to pay the money that I wanted, but Alan agreed a short-term deal with Bedford, just north of London. They were a Second Division side, and they had almost been relegated the previous season, but Frank Warren, the boxing promoter, had become involved with them through his Sports Network company. And I knew Frank, through my interest in boxing, and I thought that if he was getting involved the club would start to go places.

So Alan contacted Jack Robinson to find out when I had to be back for the Rugby League season and sort out the details. And that's when I got another shock – and the puzzle finally fell into place. For Jack made it pretty clear that, as a result of Wigan's financial situation, they wouldn't stand in my way if a club wanted to take me on permanently – though it wouldn't be a problem if I wanted to stay.

Alan phoned me immediately with the bombshell. It seemed to me that Wigan were saying 'we don't want you'. That's when I rang Jack Robinson and he explained about Wigan's financial constraints. Then, of course, it all made sense. After all, Wigan had the largest wage bill in Super League, and if they wanted to save money the first thing they'd do would be to look at the players' contracts. And who had the largest contract at Wigan? That's right. Me. So by letting me go they'd make a big saving on the wage bill.

It took me a day or two to get over the shock, but then I started to do some hard thinking. The fact that I had turned 30 and was nearing the end of my career probably had something to do with Wigan's decision, yet they knew that I was still a big enough name to command a transfer fee. I don't think they would have sold me, though, unless some good young players hadn't been coming through: Rob Smyth, a young wing, was just breaking into the first team and doing very well every time he played, so the club obviously saw him as an ideal replacement for me; and Danny Ellison, another young wing, was also beginning to make his mark. And you have to remember that you're guaranteed a certain number of tries if you're at the end of a Wigan back line, whoever you are.

First I went over my options with Alan. After all, I couldn't just sign full-time with a Union club, even if I wanted to, because I'd also signed a contract with the European Super League in addition to my contract with Wigan which meant that I had to play Super League in Britain. And as I was one of the leading lights of the game at that time, and was pretty well-known outside the traditional League areas, I knew that Maurice Lindsay, Chief Executive of the Rugby Football League, wouldn't want to lose me to Union. Of course, I could always stay with Wigan for the three years that my contract had to run – but the fact that they had said that they were prepared to let me go had made me determined to leave. And, though it would be a terrible wrench to leave Wigan, I also knew that they would probably have ended up selling me anyway – but on their terms. So I decided to be positive, and let the situation work for me.

Then Alan told me that the London Broncos were interested in signing me. I liked the sound of that: I'd be in London; the club had been taken over by the Brisbane Broncos, one of Australia's most successful teams, so both resources and know-how would be available; and it would be a challenge to be part of something different and new. All we had to do was negotiate an arrangement that would keep the Broncos and Bedford happy, and satisfy me as well. In the end, I agreed a four-year contract with Bedford, which gave them first call on me, and a three-year deal with the Broncos, which tied me to playing at least 12 games for them a season.

I signed with the Broncos on 2 August, and then the media hype began. Maurice Lindsay saw the fact that I was joining the Broncos as something of a coup for Rugby League in London. I was a bit surprised, because I knew that I'd be playing more games for Bedford than the Broncos, but I got on with the job.

So there I was. Just eight months into the year, my life had turned upside down. I'd left the greatest Rugby League club in Britain to join another one, and I was going back into the world of Union. And the way that I thought about life and sport had changed, too. But most of all, I was on my way back to London, where I'd kicked a ball round the streets of Hackney and dreamt of playing for Arsenal. It seemed a very long time ago. And, of course, it was.

2
Growing Up

Both my parents are Nigerian. They met when my father came over to London to read law, and my mother came to train as a teacher. I was born in Hackney, London, on 29 December, 1965, three years after my brother, Chike, and a year after my sister, Nina. Because both my parents were studying, Chike was sent back to Nigeria to be brought up by my grandparents in Onitsha, in the east of the country. But this was in the 1960s, when Eastern Nigeria demanded independence from the rest of the country. A civil war – the Biafran War – was fought and eventually won by the government forces. So Chike came returned home.

I must have been three or four when I first met him, and he couldn't really speak English. It was strange for a while, and Nina and I used to play a lot of tricks on him in the early days. I can remember convincing him that you couldn't eat the cone of an ice cream cornet. But he soon got wise to us. In those days he was known as 'Cyril': in fact, the name on his birth certificate is 'Cyril Chike Offiah', but 'Cyril' isn't the coolest of names and 'Chike' sounded better, so he just changed it around later on. I can't imagine calling him 'Cyril' now.

My sister went to Nigeria in her teens and had most of her schooling there while my brother and I were at school in England, so I'm the only member of my family who hasn't spent a long time in Nigeria. I used to go back there sometimes during the long summer holidays and over Christmas, but I've never actually lived there as they did. Nevertheless, I've always felt both Nigerian and English because of my frequent visits to Nigeria and the fact that my parents speak the language around the house. To this day, my mother still speaks to me in the Ebo dialect when I go home, though while I understand the things she says to me I'm the only one in the family who isn't really fluent. When we were younger we had both Nigerian and British passports, and I have a Nigerian middle name: 'Nwokocha'. But I don't think I've ever considered myself more Nigerian than English.

I always used to think of going back to Nigeria as a bit of an adventure. Once, my dad was working at a place called Kano, in the northern part of the country, and we went on a drive that took us up to the edge of the Sahara Desert – most kids in this country could only read about such things in geography books. But it was always nice to come back to England. My father was called to the Bar in London, and worked here for a while as a barrister before he was offered a job back home, just before I went to boarding school, and he's been living in Nigeria ever since.

In fact, my father, uncles and grandparents in Nigeria are part of a very large extended family, and it used to be strange going back there from boarding school and meeting relations that I didn't really know.

When I was growing up in Hackney I was only happy when I was kicking a ball around and dreaming of playing for Arsenal. But my mum was a strict disciplinarian, who didn't allow her children to mess about at all: if she told us to do something she always expected us to do it. I was probably the most unruly of all of us, and was always getting into trouble, though not for anything very serious. I spent a lot of time with my mother, and I suppose I'm more like her than anyone else. I'm very determined and will do whatever I have to do to get things done, I'm always thinking ahead, and I'm also very careful and shrewd about money. For instance, if we were ever given money at Christmas by relations, it would be handed over to her, but I always thought 'Why can't I look after it myself?' My mum used to go out and buy something sensible, like socks, but that's what I would probably have done, too.

In those days, my brother Chike was the 'golden child' of the family. He was bright, good at sport and could do no wrong, and I suppose I was the classic younger brother, not considered as intelligent or as gifted at sport. Later on he was to become a legend at school – in fact, anyone from our schooldays who read my name in the papers in the early days of my career would immediately have assumed that Chike was the 'Offiah' that was being talked about. Looking back, though, perhaps being good at too many things has its down side because you have to make up your mind about which option to take, whereas if you're born with just one gift it's a lot easier.

My childhood tended to revolve around sport. There were two families in our street that had boys the same age as Chike and I, and my first friends were two boys called Harold and Cliff. We used to have 'Street Olympics': we'd organise a range of events, such as the long jump and triple jump, and we'd run 400-metre races around the block. The trouble was that Chike always used to beat me; he would never do the easy thing and let me win a race. But because he was good at most things, I had the opportunity to learn from him. For example, I learnt to bowl at cricket by bowling at Chike, and I had to learn to bowl well if I wanted to bat because he was the type of person who wouldn't let you bat if you didn't deserve it – so I had to get him out or he'd bat all day.

Things that happen in your childhood tend to shape your character and it was difficult to live up to having an older brother who was better than me at everything. No matter how well I did, I was always compared to Chike – particularly later on, at boarding school. I knew that I wasn't going to change anyone's opinion, so I just tried as hard as I possibly could. I wanted to provide tangible proof that I was at least as good as him – by scoring more tries than he had, for example.

It's funny but we've always had different ideas about most things, including our sporting heroes. Both of us believed that it took talent and hard work to succeed in life, but my brother always used to have more respect than I did for those who had more talent than most and achieved success without putting in as much hard work as the rest. I believed that someone who had a little talent but was prepared to put in more hard work to achieve the same result was just as good. He used to say that George Best was the best footballer, even though he may not have scored the most goals or broken the most records. But I always looked up to the footballers who had broken records, such as Ian Rush, or to the boxers who knocked out the most opponents.

My primary school, called Thornhill, was several miles across London from Hackney, in Islington. The science block of the school in which my mother worked as a domestic science teacher stood in its grounds, so she had thought it would be convenient if her children went there. I was considered quite intelligent, but I wasn't really interested in school lessons and I was diagnosed as dyslexic in my final year. At that time, Chike had already been at Woolverstone Hall, in Suffolk, for a few years and my mother wanted me to go there, too. He had to pass the 11-plus to get in, but when I came to take it my grades weren't really good enough for me to get in. But it helped that I had a brother at the school so I was accepted.

Woolverstone Hall was a unique school, and I'm lucky that my mother had heard about it in the course of her teaching work. It was run by the Inner London Education Authority, and I think it was the only one of it's kind: a boys' grammar school that had boarding facilities for London children who didn't have special needs, but whose parents felt that they would be better off living in. The media made it quite famous as 'the poor man's Eton': I remember seeing an article about it entitled 'Fagging on the rates'; and there was even a BBC television documentary about it in the 1980s. Most of the boys came from London, and there was quite a social mix, because although it was a state school the parents of some boys paid fees and quite a few boys had parents in the Forces.

It's surroundings were idyllic: it was surrounded by fields – you'd wake up in the morning to the mooing of cows – and there was a church and a cemetery inside the grounds. And as well as the academic side of things great emphasis was placed on the arts and sport, and the pupils were encouraged to take part in a whole range of activities. Quite a few of them went on to make names for themselves including Neil Pearson, the actor, and Mark Moore, of the band S Express. Mark's a good friend of mine and I still see him because he DJs in a lot of the clubs which I go to.

Chike had told me all about Woolverstone Hall and he seemed to be having a good time, so I was really looking forward to going – his stories of pillow fights in the dormitories seemed like something out of Billy Bunter. But the fact that I wasn't going to be able to play what I called football was a major drawback. I had always been very keen on football when I was at Thornhill, and I thought it really strange to be going somewhere where I couldn't carry on kicking a ball about. I remember rummaging about in the sports cupboard at Thornhill and finding an oval ball – I can't remember whether it was a rugby ball or an American football, but I started throwing it around and kicking it to get some kind of feel for it. Harold and Cliff and the other friends that I'd grown up with just couldn't understand going to a school that didn't play soccer. I'm sure they thought I went to a Borstal, when I came home from Woolverstone in the holidays. Of course, none of us knew that it would be rugby that would lead me away from Hackney. Harold and Cliff are still living there, in the same street, and I still keep in touch with them.

I wasn't the only one who wasn't very keen on my playing rugby. My mum hadn't wanted Chike to play, and she didn't want me to, either. I'm sure she'd have stopped both of us playing if she could have done. She was frightened that I'd get hurt, but then she'd always been worried about that. When I was young I was quite skinny, and she used to make me take some stuff that she'd bought at the chemist to try to build me up. At one point she even considered writing a letter to the sports master, asking for me to be excused from playing, but I managed to talk her out of it. And she was pretty concerned when I broke my jaw in my last year of school. I think she thought that I was going to give rugby up, and when I didn't do so she bought me a gum shield – I hadn't had one until then.

So I arrived at Woolverstone Hall, aged 11. And in the first week of term I had my first game of rugby, and I scored my first try. Chike had warned me about what was going to happen, of course, and had given me a few tips. Even so, the pressure was on, because he'd done well in the same game in his first term.

The game was called 'Stonehenge', and I suppose it was something of a relic from Woolverstone's public school days. At any rate, it was something of a school tradition – the whole school turned out to watch – and it was a chance for the sports staff to find out who had natural ability, and get an idea of who could run, who was big and strong and who could tackle. All the new boys were taken out to the rugby pitch and split into two groups, of about 30 boys each. There were three balls on the pitch, with a referee for each one, and the object of the game was to grab a ball and score a try. With no real rules it was essentially a big free-for-all, and when someone scored, the ball was just kicked back into the middle of the field again to restart the game.

With my brother's example to inspire me, as well as his tips, I was anxious to take the opportunity to establish myself in front of the whole school, and I managed to score quite a few tries. I'm not quite sure how I did it, though. It certainly wasn't because I was the fastest boy on the pitch – I wasn't the quickest by any means, and later on I couldn't even get in to the school relay team.

But I was always in the rugby side. I played on the wing during my first year – if you're black and reasonably fast you tend to be put on the wing which is a bit of a stereotype situation, I suppose – but when the rugby masters saw that I could play a bit I was moved to centre, and sometimes even to fly-half. I enjoyed playing centre and didn't play on the wing again until I left school. And I kept on scoring tries – more tries than anyone else, in fact. For me, scoring was the fun part of playing, even though I knew that the most important thing was to win the game. So it felt like a waste if I'd scored a hat-trick but the side had lost the game; on the other hand I had an empty feeling if we'd won, but I hadn't scored. If anything, it became easier to score as I moved up the school, because I was getting faster and stronger. People don't think of me as a player who's physically strong, but it's always been quite difficult to put me down when I've got the ball – I suppose that it's as much to do with balance as anything else. Other people could run faster than me on the track, but I could run faster with the ball.

Of course, rugby wasn't the only game I played at Woolverstone Hall. I got involved in just about any team sport involving athletic ability that was going – fencing, cricket and badminton, for example. I was particularly good at fencing and a keen member of the fencing club. One year we went to Le Touquet to compete against a French school. I became quite friendly with one of the boys there, and swapped my sweat bands, which were red, gold and green, for his, which were in the French colours: red, white and blue. And whenever I've played rugby since then I've worn a red, white and blue sweat band and a red, gold and green one – it's one of my superstitions.

At Woolverstone the main summer sport was cricket, and it was taken very seriously. The matron's husband used to play for Kent; and the square was good enough for the local cricket side to use it. Mr Sadler, my housemaster, used to push anyone who showed a talent for the game – and, of course, Chike was good at cricket, so I had to be good at it, too.

I was a left arm fast bowler and used to bat a bit as well, and played for the First XI when I was in the fifth form. I used to open the bowling and when I played against other schools you'd hear the opposition say, 'I hope Offiah isn't playing today,' because nobody wanted to face a fast bowler – especially in those days, when there wasn't any rule about the number of bouncers you could bowl. I certainly used to bowl more than one or two an over. I enjoyed batting as well. The cricket square was in front of the school, and if a batsman was nearing a century or a half-century word would spread like wildfire, and everyone would come out to watch. If you scored a century you were presented with a bat: Chike got one, but I got two centuries, so I was given both a bat and pads. Eventually I captained the Cricket XI, and went on captain Suffolk Schools; and I ended up representing the county at Colts and Under-25 level.

Athletics wasn't considered that important at Woolverstone, though. As I said, I wasn't particularly fast – though people always assume that I must have been – and I was only a reserve for the relay team when I was 13. Even when I was in the fifth form I wasn't the fastest in our year: that was a chubby white lad called Mark Holloway. I've bumped into him since then and I think he plays semi-pro football. Then there was Mitch, brother of my good friend Chris Ogugua, who was quicker than me. I look at Mitch now whenever I bump into him in London – he plays in a band – and I think, 'I'll give you a race now.' In any case, because athletics wasn't much of a big thing at school, you'd only ever get one man and his dog watching, and that never appealed to me.

I suppose that's the point. I enjoyed rugby the most because it had the highest profile. The whole school used to come out and watch a match, whereas you'd only get a handful of spectators for a fencing match, say. And I responded to a crowd – I've always been exuberant and a bit of a show-off – and I always tended to play better in front of a good one. That's wrong, I know, because you should really play just as well when nobody's watching you, but having an audience really made a difference to me. I played a lot of sports at school because I was good at them, but rugby was the only one that I wasn't only good at but that I enjoyed.

At the time I never really thought about why I was good at sport in general. It was only when I was older that I found out that both my parents had been good athletes. My dad had been quite a sportsman, and when I became successful, members of the family said: 'Your dad was a very good footballer and a very good runner.' If my parents had been brought up in a different place and in a different time they might have turned out differently, but in Nigeria education was far more important than sport. That's why there are a lot of West African students in this country: they see education as the only way to succeed. Things are beginning to change, but an education is still seen as the surest way to achieve success. And the only reason my mother sent us to Woolverstone Hall was to get a good education: it was very good academically and some pupils had gone on to Oxford and Cambridge.

I was one of those kids who is always wondering about what they're going to do when they grow up – I probably got that from my mum – so I had a go at most things. I joined the Army Cadet Force, for example, but when the Falklands War started, in 1982, I thought: 'If this escalates into a world war and they kill all the soldiers they'll send for me.' So I decided to quit – but I waited until the war was over to hand in my boots, so that people wouldn't call me a coward.

I was always the kind of person who would entertain people, mess about and tell jokes in the dorm, so I also had a go at acting. Sometimes I was a bit shy in normal surroundings when I was a kid, but I had enough confidence to go on stage and not give a monkey's about anything. I acted in several plays at school including *Unman, Wittering and Zigo*, a thriller set in a public school in which a new teacher is threatened by his pupils; and I also had a part in *The Real Inspector Hound*, by Tom Stoppard. The Stoppard play could have been a disaster: because of my reputation as a bit of a joker, everyone in the audience burst out laughing when the curtains opened and I walked out on stage, and I nearly cracked up and almost forgot my lines. It went all right after that, though, and I think I surprised people. In fact, acting used to scare me in some ways – it was always easier in the dorm with my mates. But it gave me a buzz – rather like scoring a try, it really means something.

My sport and activities were going well, but the academic side of things wasn't so easy. I had to have extra help in English in my first year, because of my dyslexia, and I wasn't really interested in anything academic. I ended up getting four O-levels: English Literature, Geography, History and Physics. The trouble was that you needed five O-levels to get into the sixth form, and I had to do that to realise my ambition of playing for the First XV. Luckily, the school said that I could take another five the next year, which turned out to be a doddle. I didn't have a full timetable and was playing lots of rugby, and at the end of it I passed four: Economics, Biology, Maths, and English Language.

So I had eight O-levels in all – I couldn't believe it. Neither could my mother. She used to send the letters that I wrote home back to me with the spelling mistakes corrected – having a school teacher for a mother did have its drawbacks – so after a while I'd stopped writing and took to speaking to her over the phone instead.

But by then I'd decided what I wanted to do with my life – which was why it was so important that I got into the First XV. I can remember it clearly: I was 15, and I was walking down a road in Stoke Newington, in London, just near the library. I was thinking things over, and I decided that I'd follow a career in sport; I was going to take rugby seriously and I was going to play for England. From that moment my life was set on its course. I'd smoked the week before, and just had a bad experience with alcohol – we had a party at our house and I drank a few cans of lager and was sick all over the settee – and I decided that I wouldn't drink or smoke again.

One of the reasons for my decision to try to make the grade in rugby was that, while our school had a great rugby tradition, it only had about 380 boys. We were very much the poor relations in comparison to other schools in the area, such as RHS Colchester, St Joseph's and Ipswich School, which made it very tough for anyone from Woolverstone to make their mark. The boys from Woolverstone who had managed to get England Schools trials, such as Cedric Carr, who went on to play for Rosslyn Park, and Adrian Thomson, who ended up at Harlequins, were thought of as immortals. And I wanted to be one of them. I remember seeing the Australian Schoolboys playing Scotland on *Rugby Special* one year, and I remember thinking: 'I wouldn't mind having a go at that.'

As I moved up the school it became harder and harder for us to put out a decent rugby team, so by the time I reached the fifth form Kevin Young, our rugby master, had fixed it up so that I could play for Ipswich Rugby Club. I started out in the Colts, but was soon playing for their first team and ended up being selected for Eastern Counties. I was really pushing to get into the England Schools team, but I broke my jaw playing for Eastern Counties Under-19s in my final year. When I'd started to recover, one of the masters heard of a match between London Division and Rosslyn Park Colts that was to take place before the divisional schools championship. He suggested that the selectors would get a look at me if I turned out for Rosslyn Park and gave me a number to ring. I never made the call, though, because I still wasn't right after my injury. But I did keep the number – and it was to come in useful later on.

With all this rugby, I'd rather neglected my studies, and when I left Woolverstone Hall, in 1985, I only had one A-level – in Geography. And soon after I left, the Inner London Education

Authority was abolished and Woolverstone Hall was closed as a boarding school in 1990; today it's a girls' school. I think that's a shame, because my schooldays really were the best days of my life. I've got a lot to thank my mother for, not least for sending me to boarding school, where there was no real chance that I'd go off the rails. The school was fairly strict and I remember the housemaster caning me on one occasion and slippering me on a few others; but generally I was pretty smart and learned how to bend the rules. I was a bit loud at times, too, which got me into trouble – in my second year I won the inter-house cross-country competition, and as my reward Mr Watkins, the deputy housemaster, said I could make as much noise as I wanted, just for that night.

But I didn't have any worries at all at school, I just played lots of sport and had a good time. The funny thing is that a lot of people at school were considered far better rugby players than me, but they didn't really make it. I occasionally bump into some of them, particularly now that I'm back in London. And I often come across people who went to Woolverstone Hall. When they see me they come over and say: 'I used to go to your school.'

I made some good friends at Woolverstone Hall, too. One of them became one of my best friends: Chris Ogogua, the younger brother of Mitch, who was in my class. We did everything together: we went out with the same girls; played rugby together; wore the same clothes; and even both had silly Michael Jackson perms. Chris and I came from similar back-grounds and had a lot in common – we were both Nigerians living in London and our dads were working in Nigeria – although his parents were quite rich and he always seemed to have a lot of money. Chris was the first one of my friends to have a car, and I learned to drive in it, although I got stopped by the police for having no insurance or L-plates and ended up with five points on my licence before I'd even passed my test.

It was Chris who got me a job at McDonald's after I left school. I used to go in when he worked there and he would hand free food to me over the counter. Eventually he said: 'Why don't you get a job here? It's a doddle and you get to eat as many hamburgers as you like.' So I did, but after two days I got sick of it and I told him to tell them I'd been hurt playing rugby and was in hospital. I never went back. (I did learn two lessons: one was to keep a clean kitchen and the other was humility.) Chris and I were like two peas in a pod until we were 21, but we became very different as we grew older. Our ideas on everything from fashion to girls developed in completely different ways, and today it's hard to imagine that we were ever so similar. But we still see each other; in fact he tells everyone he's my cousin because we're both Nigerian and from the same Ebo tribe.

I'd decided that I wanted to follow a career in sport, but it wasn't easy to find the right way to go about it after I'd left school. And my mother thought that I was just dreaming, and that I should continue with my education. Dad took the attitude 'if this is what you want to do, go for it', but mum thought she knew what was best for her kids, so I had something of a fight on my hands. As I've said, my parents were from a another country and of a different generation, so they had different standards and values. But though I'm Nigerian, I'm English as well, so I had different influences and formed my own opinions. Besides, parents can give you advice but only from their own experiences – and they can't know everything. For example, my mother had no idea that if you played for a top Rugby Union club you could walk into a good job, if you had half a brain. I'd wanted a career in sport for so long that there was no way I was going to give up when I was 19. So she never encouraged me until I turned pro, but luckily I'm the type of person who doesn't need any encouragement.

Nevertheless, I enrolled at the City and East College to try to get more A-levels, with the aim of getting a place at University. But even then my mother always gave me a hard time about my studies. I remember one time when she came in as I was getting ready to go out – I must have been about 19 – and asked me for a pen. When I said I didn't have one she said: 'What kind of student doesn't have a pen?', and suddenly a huge argument broke out. Before I knew it I was grounded for the night. I can laugh at it now, but at the time I thought my world was falling in; the nice evening that I'd planned had been ruined, just because I didn't have a pen. I don't think she wanted me to go out in the first place.

But even though I was going to continue with my studies, I still wanted to explore all possible ways of earning money through sport. So the first summer after leaving school I went to Essex to try my hand at being a professional cricketer. Rugby Union wasn't professional then, of course, while cricket was – though even at county level you didn't earn a fortune. I seem to remember spending most of the time bowling to the First XI in the nets, although I know I got Graham Gooch out on one occasion. I had a game for the Second XI against Sussex, at Eastbourne, where my room mate was Nasser Hussain, who went on to play for England. It was my first three-day game, and the first time in my life I spent all day in the field. I didn't bowl very well – I remember being hit for a six by Allan Wells – and although my figures weren't bad I didn't manage to get a wicket. And when I did go in to bat, which was about eight or nine, I was out for a duck, to a spin bowler who still seemed pretty quick. Next day I couldn't get out of bed because I was so sore; bowling is hard work, and really takes a lot out of you.

At school, a cricket game is over in a day – even when I played for the county we started at 11am and finished by 6pm – and after fielding all day I knew that professional cricket wasn't for me. I realised that I could never play cricket for a living. If I'd have worked really hard I might have made it at county level, but I just wasn't prepared to do it. No matter how good you are at something, and no matter what the rewards are, you've got to actually enjoy something if you are going to be doing it for the rest of your life. So I packed all my cricket gear away in a green Duncan Fearnley bag after that game and didn't open it again until years later – all the stuff was mouldy because I'd just dumped it in the bag and never touched it again. I've been asked to play in various cricket matches for charity since then, but I've never got round to taking part.

After my flirtation with cricket, I had to work out how I could continue to play rugby.

A lot of schools have an association with a senior club – Woolverstone had one with Ipswich – but back in London I didn't really have any connection with any club. I knew that the top clubs at that time were Harlequins and Wasps, but I didn't know anyone. I still had the phone number of someone at Rosslyn Park, though, and I knew that Woolverstone Old-Boy Cedric Carr played for them, so it seemed to be worth giving them a try. Besides, I remember thinking that I'd have a better chance of getting into the first team because Rosslyn Park wasn't one of the best clubs – if I went somewhere like Wasps, I'd just get lost in the system because the top clubs have loads of good young players, and some never get a chance of playing in the first team. And I reckoned that if I went somewhere where I could get into the first team, I'd be competing against the top players in other teams anyway. So I rang Rosslyn Park, and was told that training was on Tuesdays and Thursdays. And on the next Tuesday I went along – I knew it would take me ages to get there because it was on the other side of London from Hackney, so I turned up an hour-and-a-half early and sat in the clubhouse, waiting.

I started playing centre in the fifth team, and things went well. I seemed to move up a team every week, and eventually I got into the second XV, playing on the wing. I liked playing outside rather than inside centre, so I was quite happy to move out to the wing – I don't remember kicking up a fuss about it. In fact, a lot of young players are put on the wing when they first go into senior rugby, to help them find their feet before they graduate to other positions. I thought I would progress more quickly on the wing, too, because there was less competition for places. I didn't find the move up to senior rugby too easy at first, but at least you have fewer responsibilities on the wing, and there's less tackling to do, so in some ways the positional change was a blessing.

I made my debut for the first team at home against Loughborough College, on Tuesday 19 November 1985. It was snowing and we lost, but I kept my place for the next match, against, Waterloo, and I scored two tries in that game – one of them was a length-of-the-field effort – and we won 18–4. And that established me in the first team.

The following week we were at home to Abertillery, the Welsh side, and I scored another good try, so I really felt I was on my way.

I can still remember some of those games, though for different reasons. Towards the end of the season, for example, we played against Harlequins at Twickenham. In those days, Quins still played some of their club games at the RFU ground. And I can remember that game well because the stadium was huge but empty. Although we won 15–12 and I went over for two tries, it was no fun at all for me. Then I played for London Division against the North, at Wasps, during my second season with Rosslyn Park. Rory Underwood and Mike Harrison, the current England wings, were playing for the North, and although we were well beaten, by 34–6, I scored London's only try – it came from a mistake by Peter Williams, the North's fly-half, who later turned professional with Salford. And I got a big buzz when I was awarded an England Students cap.

Even though I was doing well at Rosslyn Park – in both my seasons with the club I ended up as the top try-scorer – my mum still wasn't convinced about what I was doing. I remember that after I was selected to play for London Division she more or less said: 'You're not going.' I played in the end, but I was always worried in case she threw me out of the house, so I had a contingency plan that involved going to live with one of my mates, Chris.

Rosslyn Park always had the reputation of being a snobbish club in those day, and, looking back, I suppose they were . But I think they regarded me in a slightly different way, and one of the top guys took quite a shine to me and looked after me. And even though I didn't know Cedric Carr that well, it was good having someone there who I could ask about things – he was a winger, too, which helped – and he introduced me to everybody even though I eventually took his place.

The social side was a bit foreign to me, though. I was just a kid from Hackney, as far as I was concerned – even though my dad was a barrister who later became a judge, and my mother was a schoolteacher – and I didn't think I had that much in common with a lot of people at the rugby club who used to drink beer and sing silly songs for which I didn't know the words. I didn't drink, though I did try the odd one on an away trip and decided it definitely wasn't for me. I modelled myself on athletes, so I didn't have that much in common with rugby players apart from the fact that I enjoyed playing the game. And when you're not drunk you feel stupid singing all the songs and playing games. You think, 'What's so damn funny?' So I used to stay for an orange juice after a game and then go. But the other players accepted that, maybe because they thought I was good. Their attitude was: 'He's our winger. We know he's a bit odd but he's all right.' I was more into going out to clubs with my mates rather than getting drunk at the rugby club and throwing up.

But Rosslyn Park looked after me. They paid for my boots, for example, and paid more than £200 a month for my full first-class fare from Hackney to Rosslyn Park and back. In fact, I used the travel card that I'd bought to get to and from college for the trip, but I needed the money because I was struggling along as a student. Someone from the club got me a scaffolding job during the summer months, too, but it almost ended my career because I refused to wear those big boots with steel toes that everyone else had. I just wore trainers, and one day a piece of scaffolding dropped on my toe, which, to this day, is still not quite right.

One day I got a call from Tony Mason, who ran an invitation side, rather like the Barbarians, called the Penguins. He asked me to play in a match against Oxford University, and within 15 minutes I'd scored three tries; I collected a fourth before the final whistle. And because I'd done well for the Penguins, I was asked to go to the Hong Kong Sevens with them, in a side that included Paul Turner, now player/coach at Bedford.

I almost missed out on the trip to Hong Kong, because my mother refused to let me go – she believed that my studies should come first and my rugby second. Tony Mason rang her, and explained how important it was for me to go, but Mum still thought I'd be missing exams if I went, and only changed her mind after I'd got permission for the trip from the principal of my college. As far as I was concerned, nothing was going to stop me: I wasn't going to let anything put me off what I wanted to do. Ironically, I think that I inherited that attitude from my mum, because she's always been a strong-minded person. My dad is more of an intellectual: he writes for law journals, magazines and newspapers and often sends us copies. They're always about the philosophical side of life, whereas mum has always been more practical and down to earth.

Anyway, I made it to Hong Kong, and I loved it there. It was the first time I'd been abroad, apart from visiting my dad in Nigeria, and although I had played at the Middlesex Sevens the previous year, the Hong Kong Sevens was the first occasion that I walked around the ground and people asked me for my autograph. And although we were virtually unknown, we got into the semi-finals, where we played the All Blacks and were up against players like Terry Wright, Frano Botica, Emosi Koloto, Zinzan Brooke and Mark Brooke-Cowden.

As far as playing was concerned, I found it easier at the higher level because no one knew who I was so I didn't receive any particular attention. And because of the step up in class, I started to get more opportunities – because the guys inside me were better and were putting me into positions from which my pace would take me home. I was taking the chances, and people were beginning to sit up and take notice. And I find it easier to play in the big games, too. Even today, the real test for me is when you have to play in the mud in front of one man and his dog.

On my return to Britain, I was selected to play for the Barbarians on their Easter tour of Wales. It was the year of the first World Cup, so the selectors picked a lot of players who weren't involved in it, Will Carling being one of them – he put me in for a hat-trick in my last game against Swansea. Then came my second appearance at the Middlesex Sevens to round off the season.

It was around that time that I received a call from a certain Eddie McDonald.

3
Fast and Loose

When I played soccer as a young kid, I always wanted to play up front and score goals: it was what I enjoyed doing most. So when I started playing rugby I just switched to scoring tries. And I've always managed to score them, right from that first game at Woolverstone Hall to the present day. I know that whether you're playing rugby or football, the priority in the modern-day game seems to be defence, but for me the sheer enjoyment of playing comes when I score. Okay, it might appear selfish, but scoring tries is what I can do to make the team successful. I've never been the type of person to say: 'As long as the team's winning, I'm happy.' If you're on the wing, it's your job to score tries – and I would never be truly happy if I wasn't doing it.

I suppose that the two things I'm known for are my speed and my try-scoring ability. One does have some bearing on the other, but I don't agree being fast necessarily means that you'll score lots of tries. What a lot of people don't understand is that running on a pitch is completely different to sprinting on a track. Sprinters don't have to carry a ball in one arm, wear rugby boots or run on a bumpy, grass pitch: they get to run in a nice straight line, and don't have people trying to tackle them. Taking all the hits and the injuries that result from tackles takes its toll, and I doubt whether a pure sprinter could keep going after having suffered all the injuries I've had.

When people say 'You're only good because of your speed', I consider it something of a backhanded compliment. And sometimes, especially in Australia, I'm called a 'freak' – that's the word that Will Carling used to describe Jonah Lomu after New Zealand had beaten England in the 1995 Rugby Union World Cup – and I find it belittling. When the commentator used the word after I'd scored a hat-trick for St George in the Sydney Football Stadium, I thought: 'No, I'm just a good rugby player.'

After all, quite a few people in Rugby League over the years have been as quick, if not quicker, than I am, but there aren't many League players who have scored as many tries as me over the same period of time. In some ways I'd prefer to be like Gary Connolly, or Jason Robinson, who are quick when they have to be, instead of being treated like the fastest gun in the West. At first it was great to have such a reputation, because it got me noticed and I loved it, but after a while it became a real millstone around my neck. And since that first season in 1987 I've often felt as though I'm there to be shot at: sometimes I've come out on top, at other times I haven't.

The fact is that scoring is a skill all of its own. You need the physical attributes and a certain instinct, as well as a little bit of luck, and it's all about putting yourself in the right place, whatever type of game you're playing. Shaun Edwards, for example, was never the quickest player in the world, but he's scored a lot of tries in his career because he's a good support player. In my case, I have to use my speed and strength as well as my ability to read a game. It helps that when I see a situation developing on the pitch I can take advantage of it, whereas someone else who sees it may not be as quick as me, and so can't take advantage. Nevertheless, having the hunger and desire to score counts for a lot.

I have the ability to read a game well, too, so I have an advantage over some of the players who are as quick as me. If you know that a particular player is likely to make a break, given a certain set of circumstances, then you can anticipate what's going to happen and support him. Of course, it can be frustrating sometimes, particularly when you see a situation unfolding and you know you'd score if you got the ball, but it doesn't come your way. But when a move's called during a game it's sometimes almost a case of déjà vu, as if I'm in a dream: I know I'm going to score, because I've been in that situation so many times before.

Of course, no matter what you do there will always be critics and the most common criticism of a winger is that his defence isn't very good. If you were a great defender they'd probably say, 'But he doesn't score any tries.' And if you only miss one tackle in a season, but it's one that allows the other team to score, everyone would remember it, because you tend to be more exposed on the wing. Some people even wait for you to miss a tackle, to prove that they were right. It's never been an issue for me, though – I just concentrate on the things I can do well.

People always ask me how quick I am. I wish I had a pound for every time someone's asked me, 'How fast can you run the 100 metres?' I don't really have the answer, because I've never really raced. I've only run time trials on a track a couple of times, once at Wigan and once at Widnes. And my time was 10.8 seconds, which is nothing to write home about.

When I went to Rosslyn Park I just did the same training as everyone else, and never bothered with specialist speed work. I didn't go near a track until 1987, when Doug Laughton asked me to turn up at Widnes at the start of the season as fit as I possibly could be. So I went to a gym and did some weights, and started training at an athletics club. I can remember running a 200-metres race there once, and I came third. Since turning professional, I've only taken part in few races – and I've hated every one of them.

On each of my first two tours to Australia I was talked into racing against some of their players. In 1988, I raced Gary Belcher and John Ferguson at a dog track and won; then in 1992 I ended up sprinting against Lee Oudenryn, the Parramatta wing, just before we played them. I didn't really have time to warm up properly and got a bad start – we were racing the length of the pitch – and he beat me. I went past him twice during the actual game and scored two tries, but all people could talk about was the fact that he'd beaten me in the sprint beforehand. I understand he still talks about it today.

Linford Christie or Carl Lewis may have been among the fastest men in the world, but nobody expected them to win every race over a whole year, so I can never understand why people seem to expect me to come off best every single time. The level of expectation never seems to be the same for other players: in my first season with Bedford, for example, we played Richmond and I went round Jim Fallon on the outside – he used to play Rugby League for Leeds – and left him for dead. It's something I've done to opponents on numerous occasions, but if anyone did the same thing to me just once, that would be it as far as the public and the press are concerned.

I've got used to the fact that people have always been quick to write me off. It's often been said that I've lost my pace when there have been all sorts of reasons why I haven't been at my best. For example, I remember playing for Great Britain against New Zealand at Wigan in October 1993. I'd been out of the game for about four months as a result of an injury I'd picked up while playing for Eastern Suburbs in Australia; I needed an operation on my shoulder and had only just got back to playing for the Wigan team. The Great Britain game was only my third game in as many months. In the second half I made a break from my own 22 and Kevin Iro, the New Zealand centre, came cross-field and ended up tackling me after I'd made a run of about 60 metres. Suddenly everyone was saying: 'He's lost it. A few years ago he would have left Iro for dead.'

Considering what I'd been through, I didn't think I'd done that badly. But comments like that get you down, because people harp on about any problem so much that you begin to doubt yourself. So I was glad that in the final Test against New Zealand at Headingley, a week later, I got the ball and sprinted past several players to score a really good try. Did that mean that I'd got it all back, having 'lost it' just one week previously? One thing I've learned over the years is that you can't win when it comes to the fans and the media.

When I moved to Wigan, for example, when John Monie was in charge, I put on a bit of weight, because he wanted me to do more work during a game by cutting infield instead of staying on my wing. And I didn't really enjoy that season, even though I was setting up a lot of tries. At Widnes I was purely into scoring tries, whereas at Wigan I started to create a lot more scoring opportunities. That was good for the team, but it's not what the fans wanted to see and after a while they began to wonder whether I could still score the type of try that had made me famous. I was still scoring, but not coming up with the more spectacular touchdowns. It seems that people had much higher expectations of me, so I have to keep proving myself all the time. If any other player had made a 90-metre break and then got caught metres short of the line it would be considered a great run. But if I did it and didn't score, they would just say: 'Oh, he hasn't scored.' I sometimes used to think that I was getting a bit paranoid, but I suppose it was a compliment that the fans expected me to score every time I was in that situation.

Then there was the time I was playing for Wigan against St Helens at Central Park, on Boxing Day, 1994. I broke away from deep in my own half and Danny Arnold, the young Saints wing, came across and tackled me. I had a really bad ankle that day and was playing with it heavily strapped – I don't usually strap my ankle up, so I wasn't moving particularly well. I have to give him credit, though, because he wanted to catch me so badly and he succeeded. But later I heard that he went back to the club and said: 'I should be on more money because I caught Martin Offiah.' I believe he still brags about it today.

So whenever anyone's got one over me they've let me know about it, as have the media and the fans. But all I know is that I don't think I've ever played in a team with anyone who I thought was quicker than me over 100 metres. I've always believed that nobody can beat me when I'm on song. Jonathan

Davies was very sharp off the mark, and I've struggled to beat him over 20 metres on occasion, but I enjoyed competing against him because I knew that if I could match him over those first 20 then I always going to beat him. I also enjoyed the challenge of racing against Alan Tait at Widnes, because he had sprinted professionally in Scotland so it was a real challenge. Having players like that to pull me along was great.

I had quite a few duels in the Wigan camp, too – with the young guys like Jason Robinson, Danny Ellison, Rob Smyth and even Sean Long, who is quite quick over 10 metres. Sean would want to take me on over that distance because he knew he couldn't beat me over 50, while Jason's ideal distance was about 40 metres. But there was one session at which I just couldn't beat Rob Smyth over 50 metres. I don't know what it was – maybe it was because I hadn't been on the track for a month and he'd been going every week, I'm not sure – but I just couldn't get the better of him. Slowly but surely I overhauled him over the next few weeks, though. Jason Robinson used to cause me problems because he became a lot bigger and a lot quicker as he matured. I think he'll become one of the greatest Rugby League wings of all time. He's still not what you'd call a classic winger, though, because people like to see a wingman beat someone on the outside and score.

I suppose I'll never be able to get away from this pressure about my speed, not only from spectators but even from my own team-mates and coaches. Even though I've known I'm the quickest, I've always had to prove it to them. There have been occasions when I've even doubted myself – but then I've always come through.

As you'd expect with someone whose main enjoyment in the game comes from scoring tries, I can remember an awful lot of them pretty clearly. One try that stands out from the early part of my career with Widnes came at the end of my second season. We had been running neck and neck with Wigan for the First Division title, and everything hinged on the last match of the season when we played them at Naughton Park in front of a capacity crowd.

I opened the scoring with a try, but Wigan hit back and took a 12–4 lead. Then I scored again, just before half-time, and Kurt Sorensen claimed a try to put us ahead after the interval. The match was still pretty evenly balanced when Joe Grima sent out a long pass to me on our 22. I stepped inside one man and then just took off. Tony Iro, the Wigan right wing, began to chase me and Mark Preston cut across from the other wing to try and head me off. And, although I was ahead of them, I still had to get round Steve Hampson, the Wigan full-back, and any manoeuvre on my part to beat him could have slowed me up enough for both Iro and Preston to catch me. But I managed to swerve round Hampson, and squeeze over the line by the corner flag. We won the game 32–18 and retained our title, and that try really did make people sit up and take notice. I found out later that Maurice Lindsay, the Wigan chairman, decided he wanted to sign me after the match.

If someone asked me to pick out just one try that sums up what I'm about, then I'd have to pick the one against Leeds, at Wembley, in 1994: it had everything. The try was something really special, though it's true that you need a fair amount of luck to score a try like that on such a big occasion. As a winger, you dream about getting the ball under your own posts and running the length of the field to score, but to do it in front of 80,000 people in the Challenge Cup Final, with millions watching on television round the world, well, it doesn't get any better than that for a Rugby League player.

The opening 14 minutes had been quite tough, with Leeds putting Wigan under a considerable amount of pressure that we just had to soak up. On one of their attacks a kick was put through to our posts and Gary Connolly, who was playing full-back, gathered it and took the tackle. Frano Botica went to dummy-half, and I came in quite late off the left wing to take his pass before moving down the right. My idea had been just to make as many yards as possible, but suddenly a gap seemed to open up and I went for it. I remember stepping outside Neil Harmon, the Leeds prop, and then I had broken through the Leeds defensive line. Now I was into open space and coming up to the halfway line.

In situations like this you don't really think about scoring, but just about making as much ground as possible. I knew that I wouldn't be caught from behind once I was into open space, because no matter how quick someone is it's hard for them to turn and catch you once you've gone past them. The only player between me and the try line was Alan Tait, their full-back and my old team-mate from Widnes – so now it was a battle between him and me, and I knew that he was pretty quick. I didn't really know what I was going to do, but I think that instinct takes over at times like this.

Normally Alan's one of those players who shows an opponent the outside and uses his speed to cut them down. But this time I had the whole field to play with, so I had the initiative. I decided to keeping him guessing as to which way I was going to go, so I angled my run to take him left first, and then right – before accelerating for the line. That meant he would have to chase me, and I knew that he couldn't catch me. After I scored I just sank down on my knees and thought: 'God, I've just picked the ball up from near my own line and scored at the other end'. I couldn't have dreamed of scoring a better try, and for it to be at Wembley was just incredible.

The next time I came up against Alan was in 1997, when we were both playing Rugby Union – he was with Newcastle and I was playing for Bedford. I had a chat to him after the game, and I told him that any time I felt bad I watched that try on video and it cheered me up. I pointed out that it had made him famous, but he said: 'You've made a habit of ruining my career.' Apparently the Newcastle players had been saying before the game that I wasn't much good any more because I hadn't done particularly well in the first game Bedford had played against them earlier in the season. But Alan said: 'I wouldn't write this guy off – he's put a spanner in the works a few times in my career.' And that was the day I scored a try that helped Bedford to win the game – and the victory was to deny Newcastle the Second Division title.

As far as I was concerned, of course, the more tries I scored the better. And I'd always believed that one day I would amass an incredible number of tries in a single game. After all, I'd scored five on several occasions: once in the semi-final of the Challenge Cup against Bradford, in 1992; and also in an international for Great Britain against France at Headingley, in 1991. And there had been times when I'd scored four in the first half of a game and then recalled all the opportunities that I'd missed, so I thought: 'If everything goes right one day, who knows?' I thought eight or nine might just be possible. Sometimes I feel really sharp, and when we were just about to play Leeds at Central Park, in the semi-final of the Premiership, in 1992, my first season with Wigan, it was one of those times. Before the game I mentioned to Dave Myers, who was playing on the other wing, that I was feeling hot – I felt I was going to burn someone. Everything fell into place that day, and I turned every scoring opportunity into a try. I ended up with ten, and they were shown later on *Grandstand* and *Sportsnight*. It wouldn't have meant so much if I'd done it against an amateur side, but the fact that I scored them against a big club like Leeds in the semi-final of the Premiership made it all the more remarkable.

I'd put a couple of international tries on my list of favourites, too. One that sticks in my mind was the one I scored against New Zealand, in the First Test at Old Trafford, in October 1989. I picked the ball up from dummy-half on my own 22 and set off up-field. Gary Mercer, the New Zealand wing, was the only player between me and the try-line and I did to him what I did to Alan Tait at Wembley: I sent him right and left before accelerating to the line.

My try for Great Britain in the Second Test, in Auckland, in 1990, which clinched the series in New Zealand, was also pretty satisfying – as was one against Australia in Melbourne, in 1992, which sealed one of the biggest victories ever against the Kangaroos. Generally, I always seemed to just miss out against Australia – I'd put a foot in touch, or someone would manage to grab my shirt – but on that day it all came together, which was very satisfying.

I know I've had some bad patches in my career. Overall, though, I've achieved quite a bit and done something significant every single year I've been in Rugby League. I can't remember all the records I've broken, but I've been the top try-scorer six times and I hold the record for reaching the 100-try mark in the least number of games by any player, so I think I've done myself justice.

I've never looked at records with a view to trying to break them, but if someone mentioned that I needed just one try to break a record, or told me that the season was coming to an end and another player was two tries ahead of me, I would really put some extra effort in. Of course I realised that I couldn't break the all-time Rugby League record of 80 tries in a season – that was set by Albert Rosenfeld in 1914, in an era when the game was completely different. But when I scored a hat-trick for the London Broncos, against Paris on 28 March 1997, it was the 50th of my Rugby League career – and I felt that was quite something. There's not too much that surprises me these days, but after reaching that milestone I sat back and thought: 'Fifty hat-tricks. That's a hell of a lot.'

All in all, I've managed to achieve most of the personal goals that I set myself when I first came into Rugby League – but there's one that's eluded me. I'd always wanted to be the first person to score a hat-trick in a Challenge Cup final at Wembley, and I haven't managed to do it. On the other hand, to this day I'm certain that I scored three perfectly good tries in the final against Castleford, in 1992, although the referee disallowed one of them. I'd scored two in the first half, and 13 minutes into the second I tackled a Castleford player and the ball came loose. I picked it up and ran half the length of the pitch to the line. I was sure that I'd made history. But while the public address system and the score board were acclaiming the touchdown, Robin Whitfield, the referee, was being told by a touch judge, Michael Singer, that I had knocked the ball on before I'd picked it up. I knew that I hadn't, but the referee disallowed the try anyway, and even though I was voted man-of-the match I was still disappointed.

Missing that record doesn't eat away at me exactly, but it's certainly been frustrating. I wouldn't take anything away from Robbie Paul, who scored three for Bradford against St Helens in the 1996 final, but I always thought I'd do it first. The fact that I know I scored a hat-trick but had it taken away from me is annoying – but that's life. One year a referee rules that a pass is forward; and another year you get a bad pass. I'm just thankful for all the things I have achieved. If Frano Botica had decided not to pass to me in the match against Leeds, in 1994, I wouldn't have scored that great try – so it works both ways. And if a truly great Rugby League wing such as Billy Boston didn't manage to achieve everything in his career, why should I worry?

Still, I've got some great memories of the tries I've scored, and I hope a few more memories are yet to be made. I remember them best in some of the stadiums in which I've played, such as Old Trafford, Anfield and Wembley – I love visiting them, particularly when they're empty; it's such an eerie feeling. I went back to Widnes recently. They'd knocked the stands down, so I just stood on the terracing and looked at the pitch, remembering all the tries I'd scored there. Even if I see a ground on television, I always cast my mind back to when I played there and re-live the tries that I scored there. And when my career is over, nobody will be able to say: 'He couldn't really play.' Because my achievements are in the record books in black and white, for all to see.

4
Into the Unknown

I hardly knew anything about Rugby League when I took that call from Eddie MacDonald, who turned out to be the Assistant to Doug Laughton, the Widnes coach – later I found out that he had posed as a journalist who wanted to do a story on me when he rang Rosslyn Park to ask for my number.

What little I did know came from watching television on Saturday afternoons: *Grandstand* was on BBC 1 and *World of Sport* was on ITV, so often there was a choice between horse racing on ITV and Rugby League on BBC – and sometimes I watched the racing rather than the rugby, because I thought it was so boring. The games always seemed to be so dull and dour, with big, fat blokes running into each other on a muddy pitch and falling over. I thought to myself: 'I'll never play this game, not in a million years.' Rugby League was slow and had none of the dynamism of today, and seemed to be dominated by Hull and Hull Kingston Rovers. Those were the days when Eddie Waring was commentating, too. I know that some people say he did a lot for the game – and maybe he did – but to a lad like me, growing up in the East End of London, he was just a bit of a joke, so it was hard for me to take the sport seriously.

My view of Rugby League changed as I got older, though, and when I joined Rosslyn Park I found that the players had nothing against the League game. We often used to play League when we were training, and today I know a lot of Rugby Union players who are interested in the Super League and watch the games. I think a lot of the animosity towards Rugby League stemmed from people who didn't play, such as the supporters and committee people. It was still thought of as a bit of a comical, northern thing, though: I remember that we had a competition on the trip to France, in 1987, when I played for England Students, to see who could do the best impersonation of Ray French, who had taken over from Eddie Waring as the BBC's Rugby League commentator. Ray had his stock phrases, such as: 'Garry Schofield, he's got the legs, he's got the pace: they call him "the poacher".'

But when Terry Holmes, the Welsh Rugby Union scrum-half, signed for Bradford Northern in 1986, and got £80,000, I started to think my career through again – this time, including the possibility of playing Rugby League. Rosslyn Park had always said that they would help me to get a job once I needed one, so my plan was to continue with my studies and get some decent qualifications, because I knew that it wouldn't be a problem to get a job if I became a good enough rugby player. My idea was to follow this route, hope that I got an England cap on the way and then perhaps play Rugby League later on in my career.

So when Eddie Mac told me in his phone call that Widnes were interested in me and asked if Dougie could call me later, my immediate reaction was, 'This has come too early.' It just wasn't what I wanted at that stage of my career. But I didn't reject his approach out of hand, because I was interested in what he had to offer and I thought it would be useful to compare it with what Bradford had paid Terry Holmes. Then I remember thinking: 'Widnes, aren't they the ones who play in red and white?' I was, of course, getting them mixed up with Wigan.

Later Doug Laughton called, and he asked if I was interested in playing Rugby League. The first question that popped into my head was 'what for?', because I didn't really want to play League – I was getting such a buzz from my rugby at the time, and everything was so exciting, that there was no way I was going to make the move. But Dougie's a good talker, and he asked me to think about the idea and said he'd come down to London to see me. I was flattered, I suppose, and that's why I didn't turn him down. So we talked in a pub just round the corner from my house in London.

Dougie always claims that I was wearing pink trousers at that meeting, but I want to put the record straight: they were beige and someone spilled half-a-pint of beer over them. I kept trying to steer the conversation around to the question of how much money he was going to offer, so I could see what Widnes thought I was worth. But it was difficult to pin Dougie down. He just kept trying to convince me that signing for Widnes was the best thing I could do. When I finally nailed him down, he said: 'What you're asking me to do, Martin, is to put a price on an England cap.' He knew I wanted to play for England, and was more confident than me that I would do it, but he was also convinced that I was going to do well in Rugby League. I remember thinking to myself, 'Am I really as good as this guy's saying?' After all he'd only seen me play on television, and that was in edited highlights of the Middlesex Sevens.

Eventually, Dougie came up with a figure of £65,000. I was stunned. As a student, the most money I'd ever had at any one time was £225, and that was in my building society account as we talked. I was on a student grant and the only other money I had received was my inflated travelling expenses from Rosslyn Park.

'No. I don't think I'd sign for that,' I said. I wasn't going to say 'yes', because I had no intention of signing, but it did make me think. After all, it was only £15,000 less than Terry Holmes had received. I was naïve, of course, and didn't realise that I wouldn't get all the money at once, but I kept looking at the figures and I just couldn't believe them.

Doug told me to go away and think about it, and I went home and told Chike. He was a bit blasé about the whole thing – but then he didn't believe a lot of what I told him. But he said: 'If he's offering you that, I'd snap his hand off.'

A couple of days later, Doug phoned me and I turned the offer down. So he said that he'd come to London to talk to me again, and I thought: 'He can't be going to offer me more'. This time he brought a contract with him, and said: 'Look Martin, I've gone to the board. I had to beg them – but I can offer you a contract for £85,000. I can pay you £25,000 up front, £10,000 at Christmas, £5,000 the following June and then £5,000 a year for the next nine years'.

This really started me thinking. In just one year I would earn £40,000 tax-free – before I even put my boots on. The club was also going to give me a car, although I hadn't yet passed my test, as well as a living allowance for the first couple of years. I couldn't believe it: if they offered those terms to a young lad coming out of the Academy now it wouldn't be a bad deal, but for someone who had never played Rugby League before it was incredible. I would be set up for life, at just 21. And it was this thought that made me turn down an offer I'd recently had from Bath University, who had asked me if I wanted to go there to read Physical Education.

It wasn't just the money that made the Widnes deal so attractive, but the fact that I had always wanted to be a professional sportsman and have the lifestyle of one. Even if I could have been given a job that paid the same money, or even more, I wouldn't have wanted it, because the thought of getting up every morning and going to an office for a nine to five day just didn't appeal to me.

I wanted to sign there and then, but I was scared of acting so quickly, and I told Dougie that I'd better let my mother have a look at the contract. And she couldn't believe it, either. She knew that there was money to be made playing soccer, but she'd always thought that rugby was just something people played for fun at the risk of interfering with their education. But for the first time she realised that I was serious about being a professional sportsman, and that I had the chance to be one – she had something tangible to convince her. Besides, I explained that I could still carry on with my studies while Widnes were paying me to play. The contract changed mum's attitude, I think. She'd never come to watch me play rugby at school – and she still never comes to games – but she watches me on the television now, and has become my biggest fan. It's strange, because she often meets people who've seen me play and they talk to her as if they know me. I think she's quite proud of me.

Having talked things over with mum, I thought I'd better

find out whether the contract itself was reasonable. I didn't know any solicitors, and going to one would only have been costly, but I've always been a pretty shrewd person when it comes to money, so I looked over the contract myself. The important thing was that there was nothing in it about what would happen if I didn't make it. I thought: 'Even if I break my leg I'm still going to get this money. I can't lose.' I was going out with a Polish girl called Kristina at the time: her dad didn't like me at all, but as he was a businessman I asked him to look over the contract. He said: 'Yes, go and sign it'. But I've always wondered whether he was just saying that to get me 200 miles away from his daughter! Anyway, I'd made up my mind. I was going to sign.

After I'd put pen to paper, Dougie said: 'Here's a cheque for £1,000. Go on holiday, have a good summer and then come up to Widnes as fit as you can possibly be'. But I just put the money straight into my building society account – that made the balance £1,225. And I like to think that I've still got that first £1,000 somewhere, tied up in my house, perhaps.

It had taken two weeks for Dougie to persuade me to sign, and I hadn't even seen Widnes, let alone lived there. And I'd never played Rugby League. But Dougie was very reassuring: he kept telling me that the fans would love me, and saying how friendly the people were. He did a really good job of selling me the whole idea.

The day after I signed I watched the Premiership Final between Wigan and Warrington on television. It was a very dour game that Wigan won 8–0, with Joe Lydon scoring the only try of the match. In fact, it was such a tough battle that I remember wondering afterwards: 'Have I done the right thing?' I started worrying about whether I'd made the right decision – after all, I was going into the unknown. But then I remembered Dougie was telling me that I'd be the greatest thing since sliced bread, and I thought, 'He's the coach, so he must know what he's talking about.'

The first thing that struck me as the train from London pulled into Runcorn station was the terrible smell – I think it came from a local knacker's yard. And all I could see were cobbled streets. I thought: 'I'm moving to *Coronation Street*.' Things didn't get much better when I walked into the Widnes dressing room. My first question was: 'Where are all the backs?' because the first players I met were Andy Currier and Darren Wright – they seemed huge, yet they were centres, and at the time I weighed less than 12 stone. Then the forwards walked in, and I thought: 'I've got no chance of tackling this lot.' I'd taken the money, though, and already spent some of it. So there was no going back.

But I had a pleasant surprise at one of the pre-season training sessions, when the players were sorting out the playing terms, i.e. what they're paid per match. I remember one of them saying: 'We're not accepting £220 a week: we want £250.' I was amazed, because I already had a contract that would earn me £40,000 from my first year – and then there was the living allowance and a car – and now they wanted to give me £220 on top of it. I was quite happy as I was, but the £250 per game was agreed. I couldn't help thinking it was a wage in itself, particularly for a student like me.

I didn't realise at first that, although the players had jobs, they used the money they earned through Rugby League to improve their lifestyles. And as we were paid win bonuses, losing a game could make a difference between being able to buy a new car, say, after a big game, or a new freezer, after a normal game, and doing without. I didn't take the ball up the middle of the pitch that much in my early days in League, but I still found the tackling ferocious, and I think it was down to the fact that the players were getting paid. If you bring money into anything, especially something physical, then it's going to make a difference. And if you think there's one guy who could ruin your chances of winning by scoring a try in the last minute, you're not going to be too shy about giving him a crack. But the Widnes players knew that I could help them win, so they looked after me. I got the impression that they felt: 'It's not only our mate we're looking out for, its our livelihood.' Needless to say, I liked being looked after.

As I got to know the Widnes set-up, I started to realise that the atmosphere was distinctly different to the one at Rosslyn Park. For a start, things weren't run by long-serving club members: even though Widnes was still one of the few members' clubs it was essentially run by local businessmen, who made the decisions. That seemed to me to make the set-up more professional automatically. That was important to me, because I saw playing League as a job. And the professional attitude showed through in the little things, too: for example, I liked the idea that every player had a little pile of sponsored kit. We still only trained on Tuesdays and Thursdays, because most of the players had jobs, but we would have a session on Saturday if we were playing on Sunday. It came across strongly that success was very important to both the players and the club.

But the fact that I would never be able to play Rugby Union again nagged away at me in those early days – being denied something tends to make it prey on your mind. Then one day I went along with David Myres, another Widnes player, to watch a friend play Rugby Union: he was playing for the old boys at Widnes Sixth Form College against the current college side. When we arrived they were short of a couple of players, and asked us. My first reaction was: 'Don't be so stupid,' but eventually they persuaded me. I started off on the wing, but then I moved to stand-off, and I ended up scoring five tries. The game really helped me to get Union out of my system, and I started to realise that I could live without it. And I was starting to enjoy my Rugby League by this time, so I didn't miss Union for years after it.

Soon after I arrived in Widnes I signed up for a course in Business Studies at Liverpool Polytechnic, but it didn't start until October, a few months away. And I didn't know anyone up there, so I just immersed myself in rugby. I felt a bit isolated, and I used to look forward to training and seeing my team-mates because otherwise I just sat around at home. Sometimes Eddie McDonald would call and take me to the central heating firm where Dougie worked, and I'd sit around there instead, just to pass the time.

Once I was taken to a club in Warrington, called 'Mr Smith's', and it was like heaven after being stuck in Widnes for so long. I look back on it now and think, 'I used to go there?' But back then I thought it was great: it was even a big deal just to go to Warrington – even though it was only about eight miles away. I suppose it was a good thing that I didn't have many distractions, because it made me concentrate on rugby and things started to go pretty well. And I still knew that I'd rather be at Widnes than anywhere else, even though I was a bit homesick. Still, things got better when I started at the Polytechnic in October, because my days were pretty full and my life was busy. I bought a house, too, and passed my driving test.

I soon found out that while Widnes wasn't as social a club as Rosslyn Park, the players did socialise, but in a very different way from that which I'd been used to. It was a much more family-oriented place: the players' wives, girlfriends and families all came to the matches, and afterwards the players' bar would be full – it was the first time I'd experienced that. It seemed a good idea, though I found out later on that it can be quite dangerous having the players' wives around, because some have too much influence and it can create a lot of bad feeling when they start asking why another wife's husband is earning more than theirs. As I didn't have a girlfriend, I used to sit with Dougie's wife Joan and their kids.

It was a bit different after away games, because all the players used to go out in the evening with the idea of getting pissed, and as I didn't drink I wasn't on the same wavelength. I was more into music and clubs, and there weren't many of those in Widnes. But I used to enjoy getting on a coach and going to some place that I'd never heard of before – it was something of an adventure.

It was Dougie who really helped me settle in at Widnes. We had a busy Christmas programme, which involved playing on Boxing Day and New Year's Day, and he knew that I wouldn't have a chance to get home to London. So Dougie put a piece in the column he wrote for the local newspaper asking people to send me Christmas cards: I got more cards than I'd ever had in my life – sackfulls of them – and it was a good feeling to know that people appreciated what I was doing. And as Dougie thought that I might be a bit homesick on my own over the holiday, he invited me round to his house for Christmas with his family.

I did make friends at Widnes, though. One of them was Darren Wright, who came from Leigh – I went out with a girl from Leigh at one time – and I also became quite friendly with Richie Eyres. I think it was a case of all the younger guys sticking together. But even though I was friendly with some of my team-mates they still weren't my kind of people, in the sense that they weren't really into the same things as me. I didn't find a kindred spirit until I met up with Ellery Hanley, later on.

But we all got on pretty well at the club. When the Five Nations was on the television all the Rugby Union guys – Alan Tait, John Devereux and I – used to go round to Paul Moriarty's house to watch the games. If ever I said anything they would always put me in my place, though, because I was the only one who didn't have a Rugby Union cap. I couldn't really bring up my England Students cap.

I didn't have any problems with racism at Widnes – unless it was from opposing supporters at our ground. Of course it might have been more difficult if I hadn't been a successful rugby player, because there aren't many black people in Widnes and I might have experienced some real racism. But the rugby club was a focus for the whole town, and everyone knew who I was when I walked down the street and wanted to know me, because I was scoring a lot of tries and helping to bring success to the club and the town. So I didn't have many negative experiences.

I made my debut for Widnes against Halifax on 30 August 1987, at Naughton Park, and Tony Myler, our stand-off did everything he could to put me over for a try. But I stepped into touch on one occasion, and on another I dropped the ball over the line; and I also had a try disallowed for a forward pass. I could have had a hat-trick on my first appearance, but instead I didn't score at all. I didn't score in the second match, against Bradford, either. I was disappointed that I wasn't scoring tries, but I'd been given so many scoring opportunities that I knew I was going to do well in League: if you're presented with lots of chances, you're going to score lots of tries. But I was a bit green early on – I used to think of Rugby League as sevens with 13 men – though I soon improved. And I knew that when it was time to score a try I was as brave as the next man. I wouldn't let anything get in the way when I had the line to cross – if I had to risk being put in hospital to score I'd do it – and nine times out of ten I'd succeed.

Before the third game, against Runcorn, in the first round of the Lancashire Cup, Dougie came up to me in the dressing room and had a little chat. 'You can't buy a winger who doesn't score tries,' he said, giving me a little pat. I went out and scored two tries and suddenly I felt on top of the world.

Once I started scoring I couldn't stop: I scored a try in 15 consecutive matches and suddenly I was being hailed as the new sensation. It got to the point that I couldn't settle into a game until I'd touched down. At first it was great, but after a while it became a burden because teams would go out of their way to stop me. They'd often say before the kick off: 'You're not going to score against us today.' Even players from Second Division sides, who knew they couldn't win, used to say: 'There's nowt down for you today, Offiah.' And if they managed to shut me out they would scream out: 'You're not so bloody great.'

Even so, I don't think I've gone longer than three games without a try over my whole League career – and that isn't bad going after ten years in the game. But there have been quite a few occasions when I've run out onto the pitch feeling nervous because it's my fourth game after not scoring in the previous three. Of course I'm not the only one who's aware of this record, which has added to the pressure on me. My first televised game was against St Helens, in the first round of the John Player Special Trophy, a mid-season knockout tournament. We were losing and I hadn't scored, and with a few minutes remaining Ray French, the commentator, said something about me losing my scoring touch. But in the last minute I crossed the line, so I kept my record intact – even though we lost the match 12–10. Perhaps it's one of my many superstitions that does the trick: I used to stand near Doug in the dressing room before a game, waiting for him to give me a pat, as he'd done before I scored my first try for Widnes. I got ribbed about it by the other players, but to be honest that never bothered me.

One memorable moment from my time at Widnes was when we won the Premiership Trophy in my first season. It was my first big game in front of a huge crowd at Old Trafford, and we beat St Helens 38–14. But the biggest highlight was when we beat the Canberra Raiders at Old Trafford, in the World Club Challenge match, in 1989. The Raiders had a star-studded team that included Mal Meninga, Laurie Daley and Ricky Stuart. We were losing 12–0 after the opening quarter and were looking pretty shell-shocked, but slowly we got back into the game, and when I scored a try just before half-time we went in at the interval trailing 10–12. Then we took the lead, when Jonathan Davies managed to touch down despite a high tackle from Laurie Daley, I scored a second and we eventually won 30–18. It was a great moment and a tremendous achievement for Widnes.

Things continued to go well for me at Widnes, and after two years I gave up my studies and became a full-time professional. I told my mum that I'd been kicked off the course, but in fact I gave it up because I had the chance to go and play for Eastern Suburbs in Sydney during the summer of 1989. I remember thinking: 'Do I want to spend the summer playing rugby in Sydney for a large amount of money, or doing my exams in Liverpool?' I'd been to Sydney the year before with Great Britain and liked the place, and my contract with Widnes had been increased again, so it was easy to answer the question. I'd become a full-time professional and go to Sydney.

Even though Doug Laughton was never the most technical of coaches, he was very successful. He used to go through moves with us and talk about our drift defence, but that was about it as far as his coaching was concerned: his philosophy had more to do with putting 13 talented players on the pitch and just letting them play. Dougie loved having gifted performers around, such as Tony Myler, Jonathan Davies and Alan Tait.

And he always liked to know which player was the fastest in the club, so whenever a new player was signed, be it Brimah Kebbie or Jonathan Davies, we had to have a race during training. He always used to say: 'Everyone loves a winner,' then he'd blow his whistle and off we'd go. When we had a game on a Sunday we had a training session on Saturday morning and we used to do a drill that he called 'ten on the bang', which involved sprinting to the 22-metre line and back ten times while he timed us. Doug loved competition between the players.

What Dougie was trying to do at Widnes was to build a world-class team on the cheap. He didn't have the money to buy top Rugby League players, so he hit on the idea of signing up Union players. Apparently he believed that he'd found a loophole in the tax system, whereby money paid to someone to compensate them for giving up his amateur status wasn't taxed. That meant he could offer massive incentives, without having to pay a transfer fee.

Jonathan Davies was the biggest signing of them all, and for him to go North was really something – even I couldn't believe that he was going to play for us. Some people thought that he wasn't big enough to play Rugby League, but if you're a good footballer it doesn't matter what code you are playing. Anyway, Jonathan had only been playing Union because he was born in Wales; if he had been born in Wigan he would have been a great Rugby League player, in the same way that Shaun Edwards would have been a great Union player if he'd been born in Cardiff. I was sure that Jonathan would be successful, because he was so talented.

Then there was Emosi Koloto. Doug spotted him when he

was playing Rugby Union for Auckland, and the first time I saw him play, in an A-team game, I said: 'I'm glad you've signed him.' He was a pretty good ball-handler for such a big man: he could show the ball and dummy while holding someone off with his forearm. I thought, 'I'm going to score millions of tries, because he's going to create so many opportunities for me.' And he even taught me how to do the *haka*.

But you need a good mix if you're going to have a successful side. You have to have a hard core of forwards that the other teams fear – Rugby League is a sport in which you need to intimidate. We had the Hulme brothers, Paul and David, local boys who added real grit to the team, and then there was Kurt Sorensen: he was a real monster on the pitch, but he looked after me. Kurt had a really high-pitched laugh that always sounded funny coming from such a big tough bloke.

Dougie often used to talk about his own career, and had a habit of comparing modern players to the great players he'd played with, in what was an era of greats. It was a real compliment if Doug compared you to someone like Billy Boston, the great Wigan wing of the 1950s and 1960s, or Tom Van Vollenhoven, the South African wing of the same period. I used to watch a lot of the old games on video in those days, so I could appreciate what he was saying. Doug's always been a great one for telling stories, too, and he used to go on for ages about the things he got up to on tour to Australia, or when he played for Canterbury Bankstown, in Sydney. It was great listening to him – it was like talking to your dad really. He'd say: 'When I was young I used to go to clubs and get up to all the things that you do now.' I loved his stories: you could listen to them for hours and hours. In fact, everyone did – I once asked Ellery Hanley what he thought of Doug's stories and he burst out laughing. To this day we all do Doug Laughton impersonations on the circuit.

Despite the success I'd had at Widnes I still hadn't managed to get to Wembley, and I was beginning to think that I never would with the club. And by 1991 I felt I'd gone as far as I could with Widnes, so I asked for a transfer – Doug had announced that he was leaving for Leeds, so it seemed like the right time. But leaving Widnes proved to be far from straightforward, and I was out of the game for six months before everything was sorted out.

The main problem was the contract I'd signed when I first joined the club. In fact, there were two contracts: one covered the signing-on fee, which was the money I was to receive for relinquishing my amateur status. Widnes couldn't pay me all this money at once, so they said that they would spread the payments over 10 years, and I signed a contract to that effect. The other contract outlined what the club would be paying me to play.

In 1988 the contract system was brought in, and like everyone else I signed a new playing contract, to run for three years, that replaced the original one. Each year that contract had been improved, but when the three years were up and the contract had expired I thought I was free to leave. However, when I told Widnes that I wanted to leave, they suddenly brought up the original ten-year contract, saying: 'How can he leave when there's still six years of it to run?' What they didn't understand was that this contract only referred to ten years because it was a way of spreading out the payments of the signing-on fee. To this day, I reckon that Widnes still owe me about £20,000 under the terms of that contract. I don't know what would have happened if Dougie had stayed at Widnes. He always said, 'I would never have let you go.' I don't know about that, but the way the club went about trying to get me to stay was very different to the way he would have gone about it.

The news that I wanted to leave Widnes broke on the day we were due to play Hull in the 1991 Premiership Final at Old Trafford, and at the same time it was revealed that Dougie was leaving. I flew out to Australia to play for St George, the Sydney club, and when I got back in September I had a meeting with the new coach, Frank Myler. After that one meeting I knew that I definitely didn't want to stay at Widnes. The club's attitude was: 'If you don't play for Widnes, you won't play the game again.' And that's what turned the whole affair into a bitter dispute. I remember the comments from Reg Bowden, who was a former scrum-half at the club and an assistant coach for a while. His view was that I should either play for Widnes or rot in the stand, and he said that my name should be written on one of the seats so that I could sit there for the rest of my career. I thought that was a bit much.

While I was still in dispute with Widnes, I'd met Dougie, who had already joined Leeds, and I'd worked out a contract with them. The problem was that Doug wasn't the one who held the purse strings – he had probably been given a budget and told that he couldn't go above it. But I knew that Wigan's then Chairman, Maurice Lindsay, had wanted me from the day I scored a hat-trick against them when Widnes clinched the league title in 1989. And I was friendly with some of the Wigan players, and often went to Central Park to watch their games – they were always saying light-heartedly that they knew that they could get me to join them. I knew that there was some serious intent behind the jokes, and I also knew that Maurice was prepared to break the bank to get me – unlike Dougie, his hands weren't tied.

But Dougie knows all the tricks in the book, and he probably expected me to go to Maurice and say: 'I'm going to Leeds, it's all sorted.' He also realised that I was getting desperate, because it was getting near to the Challenge Cup transfer deadline and if I didn't move clubs by January 1991 I wouldn't have been able to play for my new club in that season's competition – and I would miss out on playing at Wembley for another year.

Eventually, Widnes put me on the transfer list in November, at a price of £700,000. It was an astronomical figure, given that two months earlier Leeds had paid out a record transfer fee of £250,000 to sign Ellery Hanley from Wigan. Almost immediately, Maurice Lindsay offered Widnes £250,000 for me, but Jim Mills, the Widnes Chairman, just laughed, saying: 'This is a player in his prime.' I remember thinking how funny it was that clubs really boost you up when they're just about to get rid of you.

I was quite keen to do the deal with Leeds, and I rang Maurice to tell him so. But he said, 'Martin, just hold on.' Then Wigan came up with more money, and I got a call from Jim Mills, who said: 'You'd better come down here and sign some forms. You're on your way to Wigan.' They had agreed a fee of £440,000, which smashed the world record transfer fee. But the day before I signed for Wigan, Dougie phoned me and said: 'It's all done and dusted. Ring Maurice and tell him you're coming to Leeds, everything's sorted.' I actually thought I would be going to Leeds, but I discovered later that Doug could only go up to £370,000.

At the end of the day, I'm glad I went to Wigan. It's the club I really wanted to join, and I think my career would have been very different had I gone to Leeds. Widnes was very much Doug's pride and joy – he'd played for the club and had two spells as its coach – but I always thought he could have problems at Leeds, because he was the type of bloke who liked to do things his own way. It's difficult to explain, but Widnes was a club in a small, close-knit community that always had a good atmosphere, whereas Leeds was a wealthy, big-city club. On the other hand, Wigan was a big club, but it still had a good feel to it, maybe because it was in a relatively small town – it was similar to Widnes in many ways, although on a bigger scale. I've never been a member of Leeds, so these are only my observations from when I've been there to play, but everything seems on a much larger scale at Headingley. The whole place strikes me as a bit impersonal, and not as friendly as the clubs I've played at.

I think Dougie suffered from having too many expectations placed on him by the board at Leeds. Having said that, they've achieved their greatest successes, at least since I've been in the game, when Doug has been in charge: they appeared in the Challenge Cup final twice; and they were always challenging for the league title. Wigan had some great matches with them over the years, and if it hadn't been for the fact that Wigan had such an outstanding team, I'm sure Leeds would have been more successful.

Mind you, I didn't exactly help. I was elated after I'd scored ten tries against Leeds in 1992, but it was an odd type of elation – it was one of the strangest things to have happened to me in my League career. I just didn't know how to approach Dougie after the game, because I didn't really know what to say. The stigma attached to Leeds after that 74–6 defeat was immense, and I'm sure Doug took a lot of stick for it. Soon afterwards I read an article that quoted Dougie as saying about me: 'I wish I'd left the bugger in London.' That upset me. I know that Doug would have said something like that in a jokey, off-the-cuff manner, and it's something which he'd even probably say to me, but when you see it in print it seems pretty cold. I did have a bit of a lump in my throat when I read it, but the next time I saw him we were fine together.

Eventually, Dougie went back to Widnes, to coach them for the third time in his career, and although I've moved on and done a variety of things over the last ten years Dougie seems to be exactly the same as when I first met him. I hadn't seen him for a while after he left Leeds, so when I found myself back in Widnes towards the end of 1996, I thought I'd call in on him. I knocked on his door, and even though he was in a meeting he said: 'Come in Martin.' I pulled up a chair, and he began telling stories: about being in Zimbabwe and looking for Ray Mordt, the Springbok wing who had a short spell at Wigan in the early 1980s; and how he'd been in Australia with Ellery and Harvey Howard. It was just like the old days again.

Until recently I never used to believe that things that happen in your childhood influence you in later life. I used to dismiss out of hand any suggestions that Dougie became a father-figure to me because my dad worked abroad when I was growing up. But as I got older I realised that there might be something to it. Going to boarding school from the age of eleven had made me quite independent, but it was always good to know there was someone there, such as your housemaster, to go to if anything went wrong. I suppose when I went to Widnes, Doug and his wife Joan took on that role for me. Together with their two sons they were like my surrogate family. I know that I've got a lot to thank Dougie for.

5
Two Sides to the Coin

Having decided that I wanted to be a professional sportsman at an early age, I had to learn how to be one. And that meant adopting a professional lifestyle, attitude, training methods and acquiring professional skills. I've already said that I consider that playing rugby is my job, and a job is something you have learn to grow into. A lot of people don't understand how you can treat playing sport as a job, though, because they only associate sport with fun and relaxation, but you have to be professional about every aspect of your chosen sport if you want to succeed at a high level – even though you're earning your living doing something you enjoy. What's more, success is what drives you on, as well as the fact that your livelihood depends on it.

But nobody spends 24 hours a day at their job, and nor do rugby players: I don't in particular. It has always seemed to me that I lead two separate lives: one revolves round rugby, the other consists of everything I do outside rugby. I've always been like this. When I was at Rosslyn Park I'd get up and put on my club sweater and tie and go off and play – that was the rugby player part of me. But afterwards, I'd go out and have a good time – and that was the real me. In fact, I tend to see myself as two people. There's Martin Offiah, pronounced 'O'Fire' – he's the rugby player; and there's Martin Offiah, pronounced 'Offyer' – and that's me.

One of the first things that I had to learn about being a professional was how to train – and it's something that the Union club players have only started to learn in the last year or so. When I was at school I used to mess around on some light weights that I found in the gym, but there wasn't any weight training at Rosslyn Park. I did some work with weights before I went up to Widnes, but once I was there I found that weights were part of the general training programme.

In the early days at Widnes we used to train on Tuesday and Thursday evenings, and on Saturday mornings as well when we had a game on Sunday. We usually began the Tuesday evening session with some weights, and then did some general running and sprint work before coming together towards the end of the session to do work with the ball. The Thursday evening session consisted of a bit of fitness work, some sprints and a bit of ball work, and on Saturday we went through our moves in readiness for Sunday. But when I stopped my studies and became a full-time player I started doing a weights session on Monday and Wednesday mornings with some of the other lads who were full-time, like Paul Moriarty, John Devereux and Jonathan Davies.

Although I did quite a lot of work with weights at Widnes, I didn't really follow a specific weights programme until I went to Wigan. The set-up there was really ahead of its time, and because all the players were full-time professionals we tended to train every day. Some teams – the London Broncos, for example – use the day after a game for recovery, with some swimming or light weights, but at Wigan we had a full weights session on Monday. Then we had the main fitness session on Tuesday; it lasted about an hour-and-a-half, and was taken by Chris Butler, although John Monie would usually be there as well. Chris came from an athletics background and the exercises he set us reflected this: we used to do things like eight 400-metre runs, or simply a long run for 12 or 15 minutes followed by some shuttle runs. It was all basic aerobic training. At the Broncos the fitness drills tend to be bit more game-related: for example, they involve running at a tackling bag, or sitting on the floor and then getting up to sprint at the tackling bag.

At Wigan, Tuesday was also the day that we had to go through the video of the previous game. John Monie would have edited it, and we had to sit there while he went through everything – it could be a pretty tough session, with nobody being immune to criticism.

On Wednesday we usually did a sprint session, run by Aylene Mills, before Chris Butler took over. This was all about quality work, and we also did some plyometrics: this was designed to improve our fast-twitch muscle fibres, and involved bounding, hopping and jumping over hurdles. Then we would go on to sprints and general speed drills. At times we used to talk about 'running style', but I was never sure about this. It's all very well on an athletics track, but when someone throws the ball at you when you're knackered, late in the game, and someone has just hit you round the head, you tend to run naturally.

At the Thursday session there would be more ball work, although there was still an aerobic aspect to it. But the nearer we got to the game the shorter and less intense the sessions became, and Friday was a rest day. We treated the Saturday sessions more as looseners, and worked on moves and ran through the final game plan.

We probably don't train as hard at the London Broncos as we did at Wigan, but we train a lot more often. We train twice on Mondays (unless we've had a game on the Sunday before) and Tuesdays, for example; we treat Wednesday as a rest day; and then resume with two sessions each on the Thursday and the Friday before a game.

Comparing the training you do in Rugby League with what you do in Union is a bit unfair, because Bedford had only just become professional when I joined the club. And Union in general was trying to catch up with what League had been doing for years in just 12 months. I know that it's only with the advent of the Super League that all the players at Rugby League clubs have become full-time professionals, but Wigan, for one, has been fully professional since the 1980s.

I think that the main difference lies in the resources that Union has available at the moment. For example, you need access to a gym that's large enough to accommodate the whole squad, and a specialist fitness coach with some idea of what's required – and we didn't have either at Bedford last season. The coach still took the physical conditioning sessions, and you begin to wonder if people know what they're doing when they're flogging you into the ground. I think that players find it a lot easier to do fitness drills when they're being told to do something by an expert.

At Bedford we trained on Tuesday and Thursday evenings, although the full-time players like me used to train in the mornings as well: we used to do a weights session in the morning, followed by a fitness session; and then we'd hang around until the evening, to do another fitness session and some ball work with the rest of the squad.

I enjoy going to the gym, working out and playing touch rugby, but sometimes it can be a slog to get fit. And you can overdo it, too: after playing against the Australians I became obsessed with getting stronger, and I did too many weights and became too big; and sometimes I've tried too hard to improve my performance and it's not worked – I've actually made things worse. You reach a stage at which you realise that you're not going to become incredibly strong unless you take drugs, and I never wanted to do that. I was always trying out secret potions and diets in order to keep my speed, though, but they never worked. I've always played better when I've just done what comes naturally. As far as diet is concerned, I just eat sensibly. I don't believe in being too extreme, but I try to concentrate on eating protein early on in the week and carbohydrates prior to matches.

Sometimes I have dreams the night before a game and there have been times when the things that I've dreamed about have come true. I realise now that it's only down to the fact that I've been visualising the match and going through moves that are second nature to me – I suppose it's my subconscious taking over. It seems like déjà vu on occasions, but if you've scored as many tries as I have you're bound to have lots of memories of how you've scored them. And sometimes I can't get to sleep after a game because I'm replaying the match over and over again in my mind – I mull over any chances I may have missed, particularly if we've lost, and wonder what I could have done better even when we've won.

I always try to follow the same routine on the day of a game, because I'm very superstitious. In the early days I never used to eat before a match because I tended to get nervous. But I came unstuck once when I was at Widnes. I was playing in a nine-a-side competition at Central Park and I think it was the first time I'd played in the evening. I became increasingly hungry as the day wore on, and eventually I ate a beefburger about four o'clock: I ended up being sick on the pitch during one of the games. Now I tend to get up late on a match day and have a light breakfast – I went through a spell in which I always ate rice – and then just try to relax as much as I can. I end up watching television trying to save energy.

Usually I get to the ground about an hour-and-a-half before kick-off and it takes me about an hour to get ready. I don't like sitting in the changing room for too long because too many things can come into your mind and cloud your concentration, but I don't like rushing things, either – so an hour is just about right. The next part of the routine involves the way I get dressed. I always wear sweat bands and tape my fingers up – I started doing this because of injuries, but now it's one of those little rituals that most sportsmen have. The last thing I put on is my jersey; even if we go outside to warm up on the pitch I put a tracksuit top on rather than my jersey, which I put on only when we're ready to run out for the game.

Even something simple like running out onto the pitch isn't straightforward with me. I used to like coming out at the back of the line of players, believing that I would score a try but perhaps not be too involved in the game. But if I came out at the front, then I'd think that I was unlikely to score but I'd probably be more involved in the game. So I'd try to run out at the front when it was a Test match or any other big game. I wouldn't mind so much if I didn't score, because getting a win would be more important.

Once on the pitch, I used to have a little ritual after we scored in which I touched the corner flag while we were waiting for the opposition to kick off. But they changed the rules in Rugby League, giving the kick-off to the side that scored. So now I touch the corner flag when the opposition has scored.

What happens before the game and in the dressing room changes from club to club, of course, though I try to preserve all my rituals and superstitions. At Wigan we used to meet an hour-and-a-half before the game and watch a video of the team we were going to be playing, and then have a meeting before going downstairs to get changed. At the Broncos, Tony Currie doesn't really talk to us until we've got changed.

A Rugby Union changing room has a different atmosphere, but then it's a different game. Things tend to be more vocal, with lots of players screaming and shouting, while some psyche themselves up by head-butting the walls. People swear a bit in League, it's true, but everything is much quieter and with less histrionics: it's a different culture. I've never gone in for a lot of shouting and screaming. I just tend to get on with doing my own thing.

Another difference about a Union dressing room is that you don't see anyone being given a pain-killing injection – you're not allowed to play with one in the Union code. But they're commonplace in Rugby League. It's not unusual to see a player being given an injection in the dressing room before running out, and usually everyone crowds round to watch. One or two players always refused them – Phil Clarke, at Wigan, was one – but most players have had them at some stage of their careers.

I've had a few pain-killing injections, normally when the injury I had couldn't be made worse. The first time I had one was at Widnes. I had a shoulder injury –it was my *acromio-clavicular*, or AC joint, which rugby players injure quite often – and it was very painful. I thought that there was no way I could play, but I had a cortisone injection to help settle the inflammation down and then a pain-killing injection before the game. It's amazing: one minute you're in agonising pain, and the next you're able to go out and play.

The trouble with pain-killing injections is that you get through the game all right but you pay for it afterwards. All you're doing is masking the pain – and common sense tells you that you're only delaying the inevitable. When the injection wears off the pain can be excruciating. And I think cortisone has wrecked some players' careers: you can only have so many of them, and after a while all you do is damage the tissues in that part of the body. Tony Myler, at Widnes, was a case in point.

There's a reason for the difference in the atmosphere between Union and League dressing rooms. Generally, we weren't pumped up when we ran out at Wigan; it was more that we were focused and we tended to think of ourselves as cold, calculated hired assassins. We had a job to do, and it was our job that we were doing. I think that this focus and composure is what professionalism is all about: you work hard during the week and concentrate on the game ahead; then you go out to put your plan into action, coldly and clinically. That doesn't mean that no passion is involved, far from it. But it's a controlled passion, mixed in with pride in one's own performance and that of the team.

I started learning this from my earliest days in Rugby League. But as my career continued, it helped a lot that I was around such focused individuals as Shaun Edwards and Ellery Hanley – two of the best captains I've played under. One minute they'd be laughing and joking, but as soon as it was time to tune in and focus on the match they changed. Sometimes I'd still be joking, and I'd wonder why these people were giving me stern looks – they'd be my friends one minute and disapproving the next. And playing for Wigan helped give you this focus, as well as a certain arrogance, because we knew that we were better than most of the players at other clubs, and we were paid more than them, too. As a player it gave you a certain edge.

Ellery, in particular, taught me a lot. I suppose he was the first real friend I made after moving North. We first met when I was selected to play for Great Britain, and we started getting on well when we went on tour to Australia, in 1988. Without doubt, he was one of the first true Rugby League professionals – he was like a Super League player of today back in 1985. He had the fitness levels, the physique and he was amazingly strong, with a razor-sharp mind; and he was the most well known Rugby League player in the country. Ellery was the first person to make me realise that I wouldn't be playing Rugby League forever and that I had to start looking after myself and my own interests. He used to say: 'There's no room for sentiment in sport – they love you now but they'll not be loving you forever. When someone else comes along your day in the sunshine will be over.' I think that's part of the professional attitude, too.

On the pitch, Ellery was the ultimate professional. I remember one occasion, after he'd moved to Leeds, when we were on opposite sides. I had a bad ankle and needed an injection in order to play, as Ellery knew – probably because I'd told him during one of the conversations we'd had during the week. Late in the match he tried to stamp on my ankle as he walked past me. I couldn't believe it: here was my mate trying to damage my bad ankle. The funniest thing about it was that I turned round to him and said: 'Hey Ell, that was the wrong ankle.' I've always played to the best of my ability, but I've never been one to try to put opponents off their game by calling them names or anything like that, as the top professionals like Ellery and Shaun do – it was never really me. I suppose you could say that the one lesson that I've never learnt is to be absolutely ruthless. But I'm just not that type of player.

Of course, when you're really focused on a game and concentrating hard on it, after a week spent building up for it and dreaming about it, there's a huge amount of tension. Add to that the fact that I've always been exuberant and a bit of a show-off – even when playing British bulldog at school – and you'll understand why I often celebrated like mad when I scored a good try or an important one. In some ways it marked the release of the tension until the conversion had been attempted and the game started again. And the crowd helped, too: I didn't do much when I scored for Rosslyn Park because I'd feel a bit stupid doing so in front of a sparse crowd.

But it was different when I went to Widnes, because the crowds were bigger and there was a cauldron-like atmosphere in the ground, especially for big matches. The fans used to get really excited when anyone scored a try, and the more I celebrated the more excited they'd get – all the kids used to run onto the pitch. It was a carnival atmosphere, and it seemed to me as if everyone was waiting until I scored so they could get excited, because they knew that I would get excited as well. And the more I celebrated, the more people expected a celebration, and because I was scoring a lot of tries they didn't have to wait that long. But throughout my time at Widnes, all the celebrations were completely spontaneous – though I developed my high-kicking step on the run-in for a try after watching David Campese, the Australian wing, and seeing American Football on television.

Wigan had a major influence on me, but I'd also like to think that I've had some influence on them, if only for introducing some fairly fancy try-scoring celebrations – though I had some help, because Shaun Edwards and I used to get together to plan one or two things. But there's a story behind the dives that I used to do in the in-goal area. In 1993, Jurgen Klinsmann, the German soccer striker, was playing for Spurs and his dives after scoring goals were attracting a lot of publicity. We had a Premiership game against Warrington around that time, and beforehand Nissan, the car company, had said they would give £50 to any player who scored a try and celebrated by their advertising hoarding – obviously, they hoped that the cameras would follow the player and they'd get some publicity. To begin with everyone was a bit tentative. Jason Robinson scored first and went near the hoarding, but when I scored, Henry Paul and I did a 'Klinsmann dive' right in front of it; and by the end of the game the whole team were doing dives. I don't know about the rest of the lads, but I certainly got my £50!

The others didn't always join in, though. Once I jumped up onto a concrete wall to celebrate, at Leeds, and it was really funny, because some of my team-mates followed me after I'd scored and came up to congratulate me – but when they saw me jump up onto the wall they all turned round as if to say: 'Forget it. We're not following him up there.' Of course, it seems fairly tame in comparison to some of the antics that go on in sport today. But nobody was doing anything like that in Rugby League then, and the celebrations certainly made people talk about me and about the game. At the time some people criticised me and said that the sport could do without it, but now it's become part and parcel of the game.

Rugby League is changing now, but people tended to be suspicious of players who were a bit flash and over the top when I first came into the game: they'd rather have had someone who was down to earth, with whom they could identify. And my celebrations were in complete contrast to the way I behaved the rest of the time that I was on public view. When I go to a ground I just look straight ahead and ignore anything that's happening around me or anything that people are saying: it's a way of keeping my focus, and avoiding hassle at the same time. And after the game, I often don't go into the bar but just get straight on to the bus – again to avoid any hassle. If I do go into the bar, I won't really talk to anyone. I'll sign autographs and be polite, but I won't be matey – because experience has shown me that if I am, then I just open myself up for people to insult me. Anyway, I'm just finishing my day 'at the office'.

Because of this people automatically assume that I'm arrogant and aloof. The only time they do see me talking is on the television or in newspapers so they think: 'Who does he think he is?' And the fact that I drive nice cars and have a good lifestyle probably bothers some people. Mind you, Ellery Hanley went through the same thing during his career, and because I used to hang around with him I think the tag rubbed off on me. It's not as bad now that I live in London, but up North, where people are really into their Rugby League, they would make assumptions about what I was like without having met me. After chatting to me for a while they'd often say: 'Oh, you're so different to the way I thought you'd be.' I'd wonder how they could possibly judge someone before they'd met them. But people do, basing their ideas purely on what others have told them or what they've read in the papers. There are very few people that I've met in a social environment that I haven't got on with. But that's because they're meeting Martin 'Offyer' – me – rather than Martin 'O'Fire', the rugby player.

The difference between the two causes me quite a few problems. A lot of people stare at me when I'm out and about, and I'm often asked how I deal with it. Sometimes you're not certain exactly what's behind the stare: it could be because they think they've seen you somewhere, or it might be because they don't like you as a rugby player. If you're what I call really famous – like Noel Gallagher, of Oasis, for example – then people know who you are, but in my case I think a lot of people stare because they're not quite sure who I am but they think they've seen me somewhere. It's a grey area: you're not quite famous, but you seem familiar. The question I'm asked most often when I'm out is: 'Are you that rugby player?' It's as if there's only one. They haven't a clue who I play for or even what code of rugby I play, and I don't know what to say half the time. Luckily my friends are fairly protective when I'm out and steer troublemakers away.

Then again, people who only know Martin 'O'Fire' the rugby player often have huge misconceptions about the real me. For example, I remember having a bit of an argument with Neil Cowie, the Wigan prop, once and suddenly he said: 'Well, it's because you haven't got any mates.' I couldn't believe it. I'd played with Neil for years and he still didn't know me. What he said couldn't be further from the truth, because I've got lots of friends who I really value: I have mates living in Australia and New York who I may not see for years, but as soon as we meet up it's as though they've never been away. I've always had a good rapport with people, although those who only know me as a rugby player find it hard to believe.

Sometimes my friends come along to watch a game, but most of them aren't really into rugby. And unlike a lot of players, who like to go out drinking together, or meet up with their wives and girlfriends after a game and go out, I'm always off somewhere else after a game, with my mates. But sometimes friendship and rugby does mix: I became friendly with a guy called Julian and arranged for him and his father to come and watch Wigan play Australia: it was the first game of Rugby League that his father had seen and he suddenly became a big Wigan fan, which was great. Sometimes people come up to me and say: 'I never used to watch rugby, but since seeing you play I've really got into it.' And that's one of the biggest compliments anyone can pay me.

One of the strangest misconceptions about me was the

bizarre episode in which the story went round that I was gay. It all came about because of a club that I used to go to in Manchester, called 'Flesh'. It was a gay club but a lot of straight people used to go there too. On one occasion I went there with a bunch of friends but we couldn't get in, because a competition was being held and it was full to capacity. Then one of the guys who ran the club said: 'If you agree to be a judge, we'll let you and your friends in.' All my mates kept saying: 'Just do it Martin, so we can get in.' I agreed, but it was only when I got in that I realised that the competition was 'Mr Gay UK'. Paula Yates was the compere, and people like Richard O'Brien, of the *Crystal Maze*, were on the judging panel – in fact, I was the only person on the panel who wasn't gay. When they introduced me on stage the place erupted, because they thought it was my coming-out party, despite the fact that I had my girlfriend with me at the time. And the newspapers and the radio were full of the story for a few days, so people started to assume that I was gay.

Then the whole thing started to get a bit nasty. When we were playing Leeds at Wembley, in 1995, some members of the Leeds team started calling me gay in a really menacing way during the game, and said that I was a disgrace to Rugby League. I didn't think that was called for. Even after the game, which we won, I remember thinking: 'I want to win as much as the next man, but I prefer to use my talent. I'm not into abusing players.'

And when I went back to Wigan soon after I'd been transferred to the London Broncos, I heard of another vicious story that was going around the town: the reason I'd left Wigan, it claimed, was because I was gay, and the board at the club wouldn't put up with it any more, so I'd gone to London where everyone's a lot more broadminded. I suppose many of the things I'd done, such as the modelling and the nude shots in magazines like *Cosmopolitan* and *For Women*, made me a target. Ironically, these things are becoming commonplace in Rugby League. As someone who's got so much out of the sport and been so successful, I'm too much of a positive thinker to be bitter. So I don't want to dwell on what was being said. In fact, I loved living up North and I still see myself more as a Northerner than a Londoner; I was very reluctant to sell my house in Manchester because I still see it as part of me.

Ellery was another person who was judged by people who didn't know him, who made decisions about his personality from afar despite never having met him. That's one thing I've never done: I always wait until I've met someone in person before forming an opinion about them. On the 1988 tour to Australia we found that we had very similar interests: we played chess together for hours and talked about music, and really cemented our friendship. And we continued to be good friends after the tour had ended and we were back in Britain. We went out a lot together, and I suppose it became the 'Martin and Ellery Show' for a while. If I was ever out and Ellery wasn't there, people would say, 'Where's Ellery?' And they would say the same to him if he went out and I wasn't with him. I think because we were so close people began to extend their opinions about him to cover me, too – and he had to deal with a lot of aggravation, particularly from the media. He was the first name in Rugby League that anyone who didn't know the sport could recognise, and he'd become an icon. He was the first League player to go on *The Big Breakfast Show* and appear in magazines other than those about rugby.

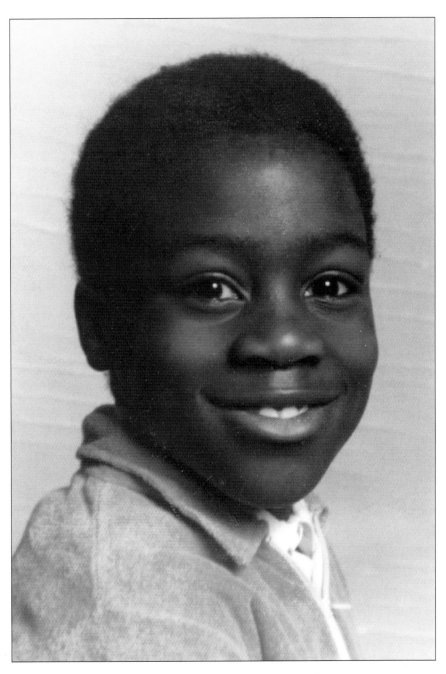

Me, aged seven. Michael Jackson, eat your heart out!

Cup Challenges

Above: *When push comes to shove, Roy Powell of Leeds gets the brush-off during the 1990 Premiership semi-final.*

Above: *League leader. Me with the First Division championship trophy at the end of my first season in rugby league.*

Left: *Try time for Widnes against Salford in the Lancashire Cup final at Wigan in 1990.*

Right: *Happier days in the Widnes dressing-room with Richie Eyres (second from left). That was before he tried to take my head off in the 1993 Challenge Cup final.*

Above: *Beating Denis Betts in another mighty Widnes v Wigan battle at Naughton Park in 1990.*

Above: *The pain game. This injury may have cost Great Britain a series win over Australia in 1990. Knee ligament damage forced me off the field at Old Trafford in the second Test and, but for that, I'm convinced I would have stopped Mal Meninga's break which led to his match-winning try.*

Above: *Saluting the Widnes supporters at Old Trafford after we had beaten Hull 18–10 in the 1989 Premiership final.*

Right: *The homecoming. Wigan fans show their appreciation after we brought the Challenge Cup back to Central Park in 1992.*

Winning Ways

Left: *The converts. At Widnes with Jonathan Davies (left) and Alan Tait, both of whom had played international rugby union before turning to rugby league. They went on to pick up further caps when they returned to union.*

Right: *Unlucky 13. I try to offload despite the tackle from Australia's Brad Fittler during their tour match against Wigan in 1994.*

Left: *Something to shout about. Wigan celebrate one of their greatest ever triumphs, beating the Brisbane Broncos 20–14 at the ANZ stadium in 1994 to regain the world club title.*

Left: Taking on the Kiwis for Great Britain in the second Test at Wigan in 1993. My Wigan team-mate Phil Clarke looks on as I attempt to round New Zealanders (left to right) Iva Ropati, Quentin Pongia and Se'e Solomona. I scored a try in the 29–12 victory which helped secure the series.

Above: *Who says I can't tackle? Doing my bit in Great Britain's momentous 8–4 win over Australia at Wembley in 1994.*

Getting my hands on the Challenge Cup trophy for the first time in 1992 after Wigan's 28–12 victory over Castleford at Wembley.

Above: *Blond ambition. I let things go to my head in 1995.*

Taking the Lead

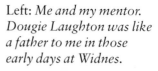

Left: *Me and my mentor. Dougie Laughton was like a father to me in those early days at Widnes.*

Right: *Mal Reilly was the first coach I played under for Great Britain. He was a hard taskmaster but had the respect of all the players.*

Left: *John Dorahy tried to change too many things when he became coach of Wigan in 1993 and only lasted a season.*

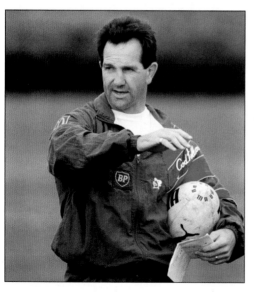

Right: *Graeme West, Dorahy's successor at Wigan. Graeme was a nice guy but I always thought that as soon as things started going wrong at the club he would get the sack, and that's exactly what happened at the start of the 1997 season.*

bove: Mighty Mal, ustralian captain 1al Meninga, gets way from Great ritain's Garry chofield. One of y great regrets is at I never anaged to win a est series against e Australians.

Right: *Ellery Hanley, rugby league's first superstar and a good friend.*

Honours

Above: *Meeting the Queen at Buckingham Palace alongside Leicester and England rugby union player Dean Richards (right) in 1997.*

Below: *Phase two of the Mad Weekend. Having just received my MBE, I am about to board the helicopter bound for Warrington.*

I was completely different to Ellery, but I'm glad that I met him because we had a lot of fun together, and I got to meet a whole range of people through him and had a lot of doors opened for me. I did quite a lot off my own bat, but when I first started going to night clubs, for example, I would have been queuing outside with the rest of them if it hadn't been for Ellery. It was a bit like having a big brother in those early days: I'd thrown myself into rugby and made it my life, and I'd hardly been outside Widnes until I got to know Ellery – then he opened the whole of the area up to me and gave me confidence in everything I did.

I probably modelled myself on Ellery, too, though like him I never drank in those days. But I saw the cars that he drove, the clothes he wore and the things that he did – I'm not saying that I wanted to be him, but he opened my eyes to what could be achieved through playing Rugby League. When I first came into the game I never dreamed I'd be able to achieve what I have today, particularly outside the game, and be held in such high regard by so many people.

I was still pretty friendly with Ellery, who by that time had moved to Leeds, during the transition period between leaving Widnes and joining Wigan, but as I got older I became more of my own person rather than just 'Ellery's mate'. Increasingly I went to different places and became my own person.

But when Ellery left to play in Australia, in 1996, I suppose I took over his mantle as the public face of Rugby League in some ways. But although I've followed his blueprint, I've done things in my own way, because having such a high profile as Ellery had its downside. He shunned the media, and he used to find reporters camped outside his house or hiding in bushes with cameras in an attempt to unearth some scandal about him – that had been unheard of in Rugby League. Luckily I haven't had to deal with much of that nonsense, but one about Chike hit the tabloids. Someone he knew owned a record shop that was selling CDs that turned out to be stolen. It had nothing to do with Chike, and the case was thrown out when it came to court, but there was a story in the *Daily Star* under the heading: 'Rugby League star's brother in CD fiasco.' It wasn't very nice, but was mild by comparison to some of the stories that the tabloids run about celebrities. I've had newspapers phoning up ex-girlfriends and asking for stories about me, but luckily there haven't been any major problems.

People often say that I come across well on television, but I don't think I'm doing anything special. What they really mean, I think, is that it's an advantage that I don't have a northern accent and I come across clearly. I think that something should be done to help players to deal with the media – as they do in Australia – particularly when it comes to interviews on television. But because of my television work and other publicity, it sometimes seems as if I'm the only Rugby League player whose name is known to people outside the North. One year I appeared as the mystery guest in the programme *They Think It's All Over* and Gary Lineker and his team had to guess who I was. Nick Hancock said: 'I'll give you a clue. It's a Rugby League player.' Straightaway they said 'Martin Offiah'; then someone asked Gary Lineker, 'How many Rugby League players do you know?' It was as if it was a standing joke.

I'm used to television now, but the first time I experienced the celebrity bit outside of the rugby field was when I started going to boxing events. I'd liked boxing from when I was young – Muhammad Ali was a great inspiration to me – and I love being at the ringside. Ellery and I used to watch Nigel Benn fight, and we got to know Frank Warren – who I'd meet again at Bedford – and the compere used to introduce sportsmen in the audience. He'd often say, 'And now from the world of Rugby League we've got Ellery Hanley and Martin Offiah,' and they'd ask us to stand up. It was quite a buzz for me. Boxers Nigel Benn and Chris Eubank were the first people I really got to know outside rugby, and once Shaun Edwards and I were in a backstage bar after Nigel Benn had fought Steve Collins with Liam Gallagher and Patsy Kensit. Someone told Shaun that he thought Rugby League was the toughest sport and we said: 'No, boxing is.' But Liam said: 'No man, singing is the toughest because they throw things at you. They even throw things at us, and we're good!'

Pele was another great source of inspiration to me when I was younger and playing soccer. As a young lad from North London I always used to go and watch Arsenal, standing on the North Bank with Chike. But after moving North I adopted Manchester United as my team, and I remember the first time I went to watch them I bumped into Bobby Charlton, who greeted me with 'How are you doing Martin?' I was surprised that he knew who I was, but then Rugby League has gained a lot of respect from top sportsmen over the last few years, especially in the North. They realise that it's a tough game and often say: 'I wouldn't like to do what you do.' I also became friendly with Paul Ince when he was playing for United, and also got to know some of the Liverpool players – particularly John Barnes and Jamie Redknapp.

Becoming a high-profile Rugby League player meant that I was invited to various events, and in particular the BBC Sports Personality of the Year Award, which I regard not only a great honour for me but for my sport as well. The BBC usually set up some kind of competition in the studio, and in 1995 I was chosen to take part in a standing long jump. I hadn't played that weekend, so the night before the show I went out in Birmingham, had a good time and then drove down to London the next day. I hadn't had much sleep and wasn't exactly at my best, and I was up against some stiff competition: Jonathan Edwards, the world record holder for the triple jump; Denise Lewis, the Olympic heptathlete; and Steve Ojomoh, the England Rugby Union international. Incredibly I jumped further than all of them. It was great, especially because it reflected well on Rugby League as well as on me.

But my appearance on *Gladiators* came about by chance. Originally, Shaun Edwards was to appear alongside Ellery Hanley and Derek Redmond, the Olympic athlete. I think that Shaun saw the wall and got a bit scared, so he said that his shoulder was a bit dodgy and he pulled out. I happened to be in Birmingham when they were filming the programme, and by chance I was staying in the Hyatt Hotel, which the *Gladiators* team was also using. Someone saw my sponsored car parked outside, and early one morning the telephone rang. One of my mates answered it, and the voice at the other end said: 'It's John Fashanu here. Is Martin there?' My mate thought somebody was trying on a wind-up, and just said 'Oh. Right.' But when I spoke to John he asked me to take Shaun's place and said he would send a car round for me later. I thought I was dreaming and went back to sleep. But the next thing I remembered was a knock on the door, and there was the driver.

I didn't get much chance to practice, so I just had a look round: I'm quite scared of heights, and the jousting event took place on top of those high pedestals, so I wasn't too bothered about getting to the final. I did get through to it, though, but I was pretty tired, and Derek Redmond eventually won. Just to prove how unprepared I was, I hadn't a clue when they asked me which charity I was going to donate the prize money to, so I just said: 'Give it to any children's charity.' I got a nice letter from the NSPCC some time later, so it was all worthwhile – but I took a lot of stick about the show because it was broadcast on Christmas Eve and I was playing for Wigan against St Helens on Boxing Day. You can imagine what the fans made of it.

I've always been pretty obliging as far as the media are concerned, because I've always realised that the press is a tool. If you can use it wisely it can be a great help, but I wouldn't do something I didn't want to do. And as you become more and more of a household name you get asked to do more and more different things. I only used to be invited on to sporting shows, such as *A Question of Sport*, *Oddballs* and *They Think It's All Over*, but as people get to know you more they discover that there are other sides to your character, and that other people want to know about them. So I've done programmes dealing with topics as diverse as music, fashion and food. And even the acting work I've done has brought positive responses from people outside the game.

All this media attention has given me a high profile both inside and outside the game, but it means that people expect a lot of me – and I've never really performed well when there's been a lot of media attention on me before the game. A typical example was the poster campaign on the London Under-ground before the First Test against Australia at Wembley, in 1992. It featured a photograph of me running with the ball and with trails of fire coming from my boots. The headline was: 'Will The Aussies Catch Offiah at Wembley?'

Before that I wasn't particularly well-known in London, but afterwards people used to come up to me and say: 'You're the guy on the Tube posters.' The build-up to the game was huge, and something like the poster campaign really puts the pressure on you. In the end, I didn't play very well, which was a bit embarrassing because the campaign had made me just about the only Rugby League player who was known in London, and everybody had been expecting so much of me. Yet a few months earlier I had played in my first Wembley Challenge Cup Final, and there wasn't so much of a focus on me because there were plenty of other big names in the Wigan team. I won the Lance Todd Trophy for Man of the Match in the game. But now things were different. It just goes to show that, for me at least, there's a price to be paid for being a celebrity when the focus is on a particular game.

So now you know, I hope – about Martin 'O'Fire', and Martin 'Offyer'. The two sides of the coin.

6
The Glory Days

Say 'Rugby League' to someone who doesn't follow the game, and the chances are that they'll think of Wigan. Certainly the club was the only one I knew much about when I took that call from Widnes in 1987. And my four-and-a-half seasons at Wigan were very special ones. I was part of a fantastic team that dominated Rugby League in a way that no other club has in the history of the British game. I can't imagine anything topping the time that I spent there.

I first came across Wigan at close quarters not long after joining Widnes, when we were playing them at Naughton Park. I was outside signing autographs when their coach drew up, and I can remember the players getting off and marching straight into their changing room, looking straight ahead with faces like stone. It was the first time that I'd seen the likes of Henderson Gill, Kevin Iro, Shaun Edwards and Ellery Hanley in the flesh, and I must admit that I was in awe of them.

So it was a bit daunting to be joining *the* big club for what is still the highest fee ever paid for a Rugby League player, even after what I achieved with Widnes. But I'd finally arrived on what I considered to be the biggest stage in the game, and I hoped to be able to go to even greater heights. Of course, being the most expensive player in the game means that you have to cope with all the hype and expectation that surrounds you. And while all I'd had to do at Widnes to keep Dougie Laughton happy was to score tries, I knew that things would be completely different under John Monie, Wigan's Australian coach. He had a team of star players, and I was just another one, though with the added burden of a huge price tag.

Usually you tend to keep yourself to yourself for the first couple of weeks when you go to a new club, until you get to know everyone. But it wasn't like that when I joined Wigan. I knew most of the players at Central Park before I joined, through playing for Great Britain, so they took the piss out of me straightaway, which always makes you feel at home. The first time I walked into the changing room, someone told me to put my kit in the corner: but what I didn't know was that the corner was Dean Bell's place. And as Dean was the captain, he naturally kicked all my stuff onto the floor – but it was all good harmless fun. Some of the players used to call that section of the dressing room 'millionaires' row', but my reply was that I'd bought my place from Ellery Hanley.

Strangely, it took me a lot longer than usual to settle down even though I was used to playing for clubs other than Widnes, having played for St George and Eastern Suburbs, in Australia. But there was a kind of hierarchy at Wigan, with various different cliques: I suppose it was because there were a lot more players from different backgrounds. For some reason I never used to see eye to eye with Kelvin Skerrett or Neil Cowie, for example – it was just one of those things. Nevertheless, Wigan had the most professional atmosphere that I've ever experienced. I learnt a lot: among other things that even worst enemies back each other up on the pitch, because there's so much to be gained from being successful.

There were some real characters at the club. I first met Andy Gregory the day after I signed for Wigan, when I was out on the pitch at Central Park for a photo shoot. As Andy was there as well, the photographers asked us to shake hands and face each other. As we did so, I was nearly knocked over by the alcohol fumes. Andy was the main character of the team, and Andy Platt was his second-in-command when it came to the comedy routines. Then there was Shaun Edwards. We used to call him 'gizmo', and you never knew where you were with him. On the pitch he was incredibly focused and knew exactly what he was doing, but away from the game he could be exasperating. He was always changing his mind: one day he'd come in dressed as a country and western star; the next he would be a gangster; and the following day he'd be a rap artist.

In the early days at Widnes, it was seen as something of a bonus if we won a big game, because not a lot was expected of us – though things changed later on. But at Wigan the atmosphere was completely different. The pressure was on all the time, because the club had such a great history. It had won the Challenge Cup for the previous four years and the First Division title for the last two seasons, and everyone was determined that the run would continue. People often talk about the great Wigan phenomenon and want to know what was so special about the club. I think it was a combination of things, one of which was the attitude of the players. They all knew about the great Australian side St George, which had won 11 Premierships in the 1960s, and were aware of the new

Australian sides, such as the Canberra Raiders and the Brisbane Broncos, who were the new forces in rugby down under. The players realised that this was Wigan's time in England, and they wanted to be a part of something that was truly historic.

Of course, everyone knew that Wigan's incredible success wasn't going to last forever: there would come a year in which Wigan didn't go to Wembley and win the Challenge Cup, but none of the players wanted to be part of a team that brought this great era to an end. This fear of failure, together with the desire to create a bit of history, was a powerful motivating force to win.

Luckily, things went well for me right from the outset and I was soon scoring tries. Wigan had been chosen to represent Great Britain in the first World Sevens competition in Sydney in February, and we ended up winning the £50,000 prize and I was named 'Man of the Tournament' after I scored ten tries in five matches – including all four in our 18–6 defeat of the Brisbane Broncos in the final. Then I scored five tries in the Challenge Cup semi-final in March, as we demolished Bradford 71–10. I was on a roll – and we were once again going to Wembley.

When I joined Wigan, the club had won the Challenge Cup at Wembley an unprecedented four times on the trot – in fact, no other club had won the Cup since I'd been in the game, especially as at that particular time it was the most important competition in the English game as far as the clubs were concerned. When John Monie was the coach he raised the profile of the First Division championship, and now it's becoming more important to win the Super League – maybe in the future it will even eclipse the Challenge Cup – but running out at Wembley for the final is very special. The Wigan players all wanted that big day out – and so did I.

Getting to Wembley in my first season with Wigan was like a fairy tale come true for me. Of course I'd played at Wembley before, for Great Britain against Australia, but to walk out there with your club in the Challenge Cup final is different. Maybe it's because of all the history and the sense of occasion that's attached to it, with the week-long build-up and all the press attention. And because it's a cup competition you've had to fight your way through all the rounds to get there, so when you eventually walk out with your team-mates in the final you feel you've earned the day. Then there's the big crowd, the atmosphere and, of course, Wembley Stadium itself – it all contributes to making Cup Final day unique.

I played outside the brilliant Australian centre Gene Miles in that 1992 Final, and it proved to be a fantastic occasion. I've told you about this before: we beat Castleford pretty convincingly, and I picked up the Lance Todd Trophy as well as my first winner's medal; and this was the game in which the record books say I scored two tries, but I think it was three. And to cap it all, it was just a week later that I scored ten tries in the Premiership semi-final against Leeds. It was very much a golden period for me.

We played Widnes in my second Wembley final the following year – it was a bit ironic considering how long I'd spent playing for Widnes without once reaching the Cup final. Although we won the game, it was marred by an ugly incident involving Widnes forward Richie Eyres. He hit me with a high tackle and was sent off, becoming only the second player ever to be dismissed in a Challenge Cup final at Wembley. Although he seemed pretty aggrieved at the time the video replay showed quite clearly that he deserved it, because it really was a bad tackle.

I won the Challenge Cup twice more with Wigan, to extend the record to an incredible eight successive Wembley triumphs. But the run couldn't go on for ever, of course – it was just that none of us wanted to be in the team when it ended.

The funny thing is that there was invariably one game on the road to Wembley that we should have lost – I always felt that when we were eventually beaten it wouldn't be by one of the big clubs, such as St Helens, but we'd lose a game we were expected to win. And we'd had some close shaves: I remember that we really struggled in the third round at St Helens in 1992, after both Martin Dermott and Steve Hampson were injured and I was hobbling around with a pulled hamstring. We should have lost the game, but we hung on to win 13–6; I also remember the game at Halifax in 1993, when Joe Lydon popped over a drop goal really late in the game to win it 19–18. The following year we were drawn against Hull in the fifth round, and we were trailing 21–2 at one point. But we came back to edge in front by 22–21, and Paul Eastwood, the Hull winger, missed a penalty that would have won the game for them in the dying seconds. We always seemed to be more vulnerable in the early rounds, but as we got nearer to Wembley we seemed less likely to lose, because the bigger the game the more fired up we were.

Then came the fifth round tie against Salford, on 11 February 1996. We knew it was going to be tricky, because they had a lot of ex-Wigan players in their side and they were coached by Andy Gregory, who had been a hero at Central Park during his time as Wigan's scrum-half. We had a two-week break before the game, and Graeme West, who was our coach at the time, decided to give us a week off. Some of the players went off to Tenerife on holiday, and I would have joined them had it not been for some other commitments.

The players who went to Tenerife had problems on the return journey: their flight was delayed by bad weather and they ended up being re-directed to Newcastle. By the time the whole squad re-assembled it was Wednesday, and we had just four days to prepare for the game. Normally we'd have a full week, and I remember thinking, 'This is the Challenge Cup. We're just not giving ourselves enough time to prepare properly.' Of course it's easy to make judgements in hindsight, and when Westie made his decision we'd just completed a great season in which we'd retained both the Challenge Cup and the league title and won the Regal Trophy competition. We'd worked hard and he was giving us a bit of a reward – but maybe we were a bit too relaxed when we came back.

For me, the game went by like a dream: it's a feeling I've had when we've been losing before in big matches and what's happening just doesn't seem real. David Young, Salford's captain, scored first, but we came back strongly and went close to scoring on several occasions – but we couldn't get the ball over the try line. Then Salford went into a 14–0 lead, with a try by Scott Naylor and three goals from Steve Blakeley. Just before half-time, Va'aiga Tuigamala gave us some hope with a try, but just after the interval Naylor scored his second try. And although I managed to score under the posts, Salford came back at us again, and a try by Scott Martin put them 26–10 ahead with just 11 minutes remaining. We tried everything in those dying minutes, and although Tuigamala scored another try just before the final whistle it wasn't enough. We lost 26–16. After nine years and 44 games, Wigan's tremendous C\up run was over.

All that was going through my mind during the game was: 'We can't lose, we can't lose.' We did, though, yet even at full-time it was hard believe to it. Everyone in the dressing room afterwards was shell-shocked, but we were still pretty professional about it, reminding ourselves that there was still the Super League title to go for and the Premiership as well. I think that we were pretty positive, and we tried not to dwell on the defeat for too long – partly because nobody, apart from Shaun, had played in all the cup ties over the nine-year run. I'd been there quite a while, yet I'd only played in four of the cup runs and many of that team had played in fewer than that. I wouldn't go so far as to call it relief, but there was also a feeling that the immense pressure that had been on us to keep winning had been lifted by the defeat.

I suppose it was good for Rugby League to have two new teams in the final, too, and St Helens were no doubt pleased that someone had done the job of beating Wigan for them – they'd always found it so difficult to do. But it really hurt when I saw St Helens and Bradford walking out at Wembley in May. I was in the BBC studio as part of their commentary team – I watched finals many times from there during my years with Widnes.

If the 1996 cup campaign marked one of the low points of my time at Wigan, beating the Brisbane Broncos in Brisbane, in 1994, to win the World Club Challenge was certainly one of the highlights. Wigan pioneered these games against the Australian champions when they beat Manly at Central Park, in 1987, and British clubs had won all the subsequent clashes until we faced the Brisbane Broncos at Central Park, in 1992, and were beaten 22–8. In 1994, we were to take them on again, but this on their home ground – it was the first time that a British team had gone to Australia to take on their champions.

The match was scheduled for 1 June, and we flew out to Brisbane a week before the game. Our domestic season was over and despite another tough campaign we had won the Challenge Cup, the First Division Championship and the Premiership Trophy, so for the first few days in Brisbane we relaxed and enjoyed ourselves. We only really got into our training in the second half of the week, so the prospect of being humiliated by a world-class Broncos side was a very real one. I remember thinking that we wouldn't be able to hold our heads up when we got back to Britain if we lost heavily, so pride was a big motivating factor, and by the time the match came round we were really fired up.

English teams have always been noted for their attacking capabilities, but we knew we had to compete well in defence and match the Broncos in intensity all the way if we were to have any chance of winning the game. Over the years, British teams have tried to beat the Australians at their own game, by aiming to play error-free football, but it's never really worked. My view is that you've got to combine the natural flair of the British game with a much tighter defence – and that's just what we did against the Broncos that day. We showed our creativity in attack, we didn't make too many mistakes and we ended up with a fantastic 20–14 win. Beating a top team like the Broncos on their own patch was a tremendous achievement, and being the first British club to win the World Club Challenge away from home was typical of the way that Wigan have been trailblazers for the game.

A lot of Wigan's achievements can be put down to the fact that they had the best players and the best set-up. I suppose it all began in the mid-1980s, when they were prepared to smash transfer fee records to bring the best players in the country to the club. Ellery Hanley was the first – he was signed from Bradford Northern for a record £85,000 – then came Joe Lydon, for £100,000, Andy Gregory for £130,000, and finally there was my transfer from Widnes. And as well as buying good players, the club was to bring on home-grown talent, such as Shaun Edwards.

Great players like Ellery Hanley, Kevin Iro and Andy Gregory would have been successful in whatever team they played, but I believe that being with Wigan helped them to even greater successes. And aside from the big-name players, there were people like Sam Panapa, Billy McGinty and Neil Cowie who wouldn't have been considered the best players in the world when they first came to Wigan, but who ended up playing at a level so high that it would have been unthinkable at their old clubs.

It's hard to say which is the best team I played in at Wigan, but the sides of 1992 and 1994 would take some beating. And of all the centres I've played with, Gene Miles was the best. I only played with him for half a season, in 1992, but that short time was probably the most successful period of my life. We used to call Gene 'Big Red', and I loved playing outside him. When we played touch rugby in training he was so lazy that he used to play on the wing and never wanted to run,: it all seemed like too much effort for him. But on match days he was the supreme centre. I was never the type who could dodge and weave, like Jason Robinson, nor was I big and strong, so playing alongside Gene was ideal for me: he was a big centre who could suck in tacklers before feeding me the ball, and I just knew that if he broke through and I was on his shoulder I would score.

Of course not every player was suited to the regime at Wigan, and a number of players moved on having failed to fit in and make their mark. Everything was just right at Wigan, from the coaching staff through to Maurice Lindsay, the Chairman. I wasn't there during Graham Lowe's time as coach, in the 1980s, but I'm sure that he laid the foundation for the club's success by concentrating on fitness and conditioning. He was the man who set up a proper weights room, so that the players could do the type of training that Australian players had been doing for years. And John Monie built on his ideas when he took over as coach.

But a good deal of Wigan's success was down to Maurice Lindsay, who had joined the board in 1980 at the lowest point in the club's fortunes, when it had been relegated to the Second Division for the first time in its history. Maurice set about re-vitalising Wigan by streamlining the board and running the club strictly on business lines. He also started to get the right people involved in the club, from players and coaches down to the people who worked in the offices, such as club secretary Mary Charnock and her assistant Mandy Roper. They looked after me so well while I was there that I sent them flowers and chocolates when I left. Then there's Taff, the head groundsman and kit man – even though the players give him stick about their boots, he's vital to the running of the place. It's not just about the players: everyone involved is part of the Wigan success story.

As far as the players were concerned they were in a highly professional environment and were treated properly, and they behaved accordingly. Once you see the rewards that are on offer if you are successful, you work hard. Everyone was pushing in the right direction, and the fact that the whole club was so focused made Wigan really hard to beat. And sometimes the team ended up winning even when it hadn't played particularly well, because there's this strong sense of purpose.

Another thing that was new to me when I arrived at Wigan was the training regime. At Widnes, we trained on Tuesday and Thursday evenings and a had lighter session on Saturday morning if we had a game on Sunday. At Wigan the programme was much more structured: we trained every day, because all the players were full-time, and there were special sessions on sprinting and weights as well as the usual team sessions. And we had experts to supervise us: when I first joined, for example, Bill Hartley, the former Olympic athlete, was responsible for general fitness training and sprint work.

At some clubs, everyone in the squad has to attend every session, every week – you're virtually clocking in and clocking out. But they didn't need to be so heavy-handed at Wigan, because the players wanted to do the work: they had the right attitude. And everything we did involved a lot of competition:

for example, if Andy Platt, the prop, could bench-press the heaviest weight, everyone would try to outdo him. It helped all round – I certainly found it easier to do my sprint work when the other players were all pushing me by trying to beat me. It makes such a difference when players don't have to be told what to do, and it became obvious that was the case as soon as I arrived.

After a while, Wigan became to Rugby League what Liverpool had been to soccer in the 1970s. If you've got the right structure in place you can swap personnel and it won't affect things too much. So you can substitute Ellery Hanley for Martin Offiah, for example, or Gene Miles for Kevin Iro – or even Jack Robinson for Maurice Lindsay as chairman. It doesn't make much difference. When Wigan got rid of me, a lot of people made a fuss, but I said: 'Haven't you seen all this before?'. The same thing had happened when they got rid of Ellery, Kevin Iro and all the others.

John Monie was the coach at Wigan when I arrived, and he was very different to Doug Laughton. He wasn't nearly as tolerant or as sympathetic as Doug, and took the view that because he had great players he wouldn't accept anything less than greatness from any of them.

John used to edit a video of the things in Sunday's game that he wanted to highlight and go through it with us at our Tuesday sessions. Sometimes the points were positive, but often they were mistakes that had been made – and if someone had made a major blunder in a game he would be given a really hard time. A lot of players used to have nightmares about these sessions. And sometimes John would use reverse psychology, so if you played really well he would tell you played badly – and sometimes if you played really badly he'd say you played well. He was quick to cut anyone who was getting big-headed down to size, but sometimes he would pick you up if you played really badly and were depressed about it by saying: 'Let's look at the good points.'

It didn't matter who you were or how long you had been at the club, nobody escaped John's criticism – from Andy Platt to Dean Bell. I remember one occasion when John turned to Gene Miles and said: 'That's Z-grade stuff, Gene.' And you can't get much lower than that. Naturally, I didn't escape. For instance, after we'd beaten Bradford 71–10 in the semi-final of the Challenge Cup, in 1992, and I'd scored five tries, John asked to see me after training. He said, 'Martin, apart from the five tries you scored you didn't do anything in the game.' I couldn't believe it. I really didn't know whether he was joking or not. But I don't think he was, and when I told Dave Myers, the other Wigan winger at the time, about it, he didn't think so either.

Mind you, Monie's tactics worked. At the end of that season we played St Helens in the Premiership final at Old Trafford, a week after I'd scored my ten tries against Leeds in the semi-final. At half-time we were losing 12–10, and he really laid into us in the dressing room; he turned to me and said: 'You can't be brilliant one week and shit the next. I'm just not having that from you.' I went out and scored two tries, and we ended up winning 48–16.

The one time the Wigan system broke down when I was there was when John Monie left after the 1992/93 season and was replaced by John Dorahy, another Australian. He only lasted a season, and his main problem was that he tried to change too many things. There's an old adage 'if it's not broken don't fix it', and when you have just come through a period of great success, as we had under John Monie, the last thing you need is to hold a two-hour session every day to try to change the moves that have brought you that success. I wasn't playing at the start of that 1993/94 season, because I'd injured my shoulder playing in Australia during the summer, so I watched what was happening from the sidelines.

The discontent set in pretty much before the season had kicked off. The players became resentful about the training sessions, and Dorahy also rubbed Shaun Edwards up the wrong way. Shaun had been a major influence on the team for many years, and a lot of the players respected him and his views – even though they might not agree with him. John Dorahy blamed him once on television for losing a game, saying: 'We would have won if certain people had done what I told them to do.' He didn't name names, but all the players knew that he was referring to Shaun.

He brought in a lot of new ideas, too: he told us how he wanted us to run with the ball; and talked about how you should run at your opponent's inside shoulder when you're making a break. It was all getting too technical, because Wigan had always played simple rugby – the players weren't into complex moves at all. Wigan didn't beat teams by introducing a fantastic new move – a lot of the time they just stole ideas from other teams and improved their execution. When Brian Smith was coaching at Bradford, for example, he came up with the idea of attacking the blindside. We picked up on this and developed it – Shaun is very good at doing this, as are John

Monie and Graeme West. When it comes down to it, Rugby League is a very simple game. What wins matches is fitness, work-rate and execution. There was no secret about the Wigan moves because a lot of them were used by Great Britain, but even if the opposition knew what was happening they couldn't do anything about it because our execution was so good. A lot of coaches – Mike McClennan when he was at St Helens, for example – used to bring in fancy ideas, such as heading the ball over the line from a free kick. You might get a try, but you're not going to win a championship by focusing on ridiculous things like that. What wins titles and trophies is excellence in the execution of your basic plays – and that's what Wigan were so good at. So I believe that John Dorahy made a big mistake by trying to make such radical changes.

Personally, I quite liked John. But I thought it was unjustified and quite unfair when he dropped both Shaun and I from the Wigan team. It was the first time I'd ever been dropped in my Rugby League career, and only the second time I'd played in the A-team, the first being when I was in dispute at Widnes.

It was October 1993, and I was just coming back into the side after a shoulder injury. After a couple of games for Wigan, against Leigh and Halifax, I was selected to play for Great Britain in the Second Test against New Zealand, at Central Park. I scored in the game, and was picked for the side for the Third Test at Headingley the following week.

Now you have to understand that, because Rugby League games are normally played on Sunday, the players don't really have weekends: you can't really go out on Friday night or Saturday night. But it was great when we had a game on Friday night, because we knew that if we won we could go out and have a good time and then enjoy Saturday night as well. The Wigan coaches always understood this and respected the players' professionalism, and were never afraid to give them time off. If we had a big win on a Friday under Graeme West, for example, he'd often say: 'See you Monday morning.' Effectively he was giving us a day off. So there'd be a big roar because everyone was on win money, we'd done well and we could enjoy ourselves. And we still had a whole week to prepare for the next game, so there wasn't a problem.

But John Dorahy went about things in a completely different way. He had a habit of calling us in for training at ridiculous times, such as 8 o'clock on Sunday or Monday morning. The players still turned up, of course, because it's their job to do so; but they really resented it. Another of his favourite tricks was to make us go and watch other teams – so after a training session we'd all troop off to somewhere like St Helens. Like a lot of the other players I didn't like doing this: I didn't mind going to other grounds to play, because I knew that at least I was getting paid for any abuse that the crowd might dish out, but I didn't see why I should have to sit in the crowd and be given a hard time while watching two other teams.

Anyway, on the weekend that Shaun and I were playing for Great Britain in the Third Test, John arranged for the players to watch St Helens playing Bradford on the Sunday. Shaun and I didn't know about this, so after the game at Leeds we drove to Southport for a soul weekend. We'd just won a Test series and felt like having a good time.

But Dorahy dropped both of us for the next Wigan game because we hadn't joined the rest of the team to watch the match at Bradford. I did explain that we hadn't known about the arrangement because we'd been in camp with Great Britain for most of the week, but he said that I should have rung the club and found out what was happening. He told me that he understood what I was saying, but that he had to be seen to be taking action.

I just didn't think it was that important an issue. I could understand it if I'd missed training on the Saturday and we had a game on the Sunday, but this was completely different. He could have given me a bit of leeway, but he was having a bit of a problem with some players so he had to make an example: I felt that Shaun and I were being made scapegoats. But I accepted his decision, and I always gave him the utmost respect, unlike some players. And, again unlike some players, I never went over his head to speak to the Chairman – I'd never do that. And even though I thought he was wrong, I still went out and played in the A-team, though the first team lost and we were back in the side for the next game.

Then came the debacle against Castleford in the Regal Trophy final, when we got hammered 33–2. Dorahy had made a big point of dropping Andy Farrell and Neil Cowie at the start of the week, but then brought them back for some reason – it was hardly the ideal preparation for the game.

Dorahy was losing the respect of the players, and towards the end of the season it became obvious that something had to be done. On one occasion Dean Bell took charge of coaching, but Dorahy stayed around, giving advice. Dean found he couldn't work under such conditions, and although Dorahy was back in charge in theory, the players just did their own thing in practice. We went back to the old moves and everyone began to feel more comfortable – and that's what turned the season around and made it so successful for us. The reason that Wigan won the league and the Challenge Cup was that the players took control. In fact, Shaun Edwards was more or less Wigan's coach during this time – he's fulfilled the role on and off for a few years anyway, which is why he's had a tough time with some coaches.

John Dorahy left Wigan soon after the Challenge Cup Final, and Graeme West took over in time for the Premiership Final before taking us to Australia for the World Club Challenge match against the Brisbane Broncos. He had been at the club a long time as a player, as coach to the A-team and in various other capacities. Westie was a nice guy and everyone liked him, and I didn't have too many problems with him on the whole. But he was probably too nice, and when he first got the job everyone knew that sooner or later he'd be sacked. That might sound harsh, but it's exactly what happened when Wigan made a poor start to the 1997 season. I think Westie had been around the club too long, and though the players all liked him they didn't really have sufficient respect for him –players never have any respect for the A-team coach anyway, because no one wants to play in the second team. And Wigan didn't really need a coach at the time, because Shaun was more or less taking care of that side of things.

Westie tried to exert his authority after a while, but by then it was too late: things were on a downhill slide, and people just resent you if you change and try to be hard later on in your tenure rather than at the outset. And as soon as things started to go wrong it was obvious that he was going to be made a scapegoat.

One of the things I enjoyed most about my time at Wigan was watching the younger players come into the side and develop, both as players and people. Kris Radlinski was another talented youngster who came through during my time there. He missed out on a place on the Great Britain Academy tour so rather than mope around he worked very, very hard during the summer to build up a lot of power and speed. His game improved no end, and he eventually overtook all those who went on the tour and gained full international honours. If you can get a place in the Wigan team and keep it, national recognition is almost bound to follow because the standard at the club is so high.

I also saw Jason Robinson grow from a raw kid, fresh out of the Academy, into one of the greatest players in the world – and it's not just as a rugby player that he's matured. When he first came into the team he wouldn't say boo to a goose in the changing room, but as his confidence grew he suddenly turned into a brash, arrogant, cocky young man. At one stage, his best mates in the team were Kelvin Skerrett and Neil Cowie, and they formed a little gang that used to go out and get drunk during the week. Jason would be drinking, womanising and swearing with the rest of them.

Then Va'aiga Tuigamala (Inga) came into the team and Jason became an entirely different person. He's quite a devout Christian now, and he's matured into a concerned adult who is a pillar of society.

Inga was a major signing for the club, and some people seemed to think that I'd be worried about keeping my place in the team – he was a winger, after all, and with Jason Robinson around as well Wigan had three wingers vying for two places.

But I always told people that I'd rather have Inga in my team than have to play against him. I've always been confident of my own abilities, and never been frightened of other players coming into the team, but it's hard to ignore it when everyone is telling you you're on your way out of the club. As it turned out, though, Inga played centre and someone else had to make way for him.

Inga didn't just make his mark on the field at Wigan. He was a devout Christian, and everybody around him was aware of it. For some unknown reason there used to be a Bible in the physio room – maybe they thought that they might have to give someone the last rites – and sometimes you'd find Inga in there reading it when you went in for treatment. So religion automatically became a topic of conversation in the changing room. I joined in – I believe in God but I wouldn't say I was particularly religious, and it's only natural to ask questions. People used to say to him, 'All right, explain that to me,' or 'What about this?'

Though Inga would never push his religion down anyone's throat, he's perfectly happy to discuss things openly, and that's why Jason Robinson is a born-again Christian today. People like Apollo Perelini, the St Helens prop, and other players who were Christians used to meet at a house in Wigan and have barbecues – I went along once.

I would have been happy to stay at Wigan a bit longer, but I'm a realist: I'd had my time there and it was the moment to move on. But, meaning no disrespect to Bedford or to the London Broncos, I realised that wherever I went it was never going to be the same as playing at Wigan during those glory days.

So when my new deals had been signed, I got on with the practical side of severing my ties with Wigan and moving to London. But the day the news of my transfer to the London Broncos broke in the newspapers, I got a phone call from Alan McColm, my agent, who said there would be a lot of reporters around the club and suggested that it might be best if I stayed away from Wigan for a while. So I didn't go near the club for about a week, and when I eventually went back to collect my gear I made sure I picked a time when there wouldn't be many people around.

I ended up having a little walk around the place and allowed myself to reflect on the good times I'd had there and what I'd achieved. I've never been strong on sentiment – Ellery taught me that you can't be when you're a professional sportsman – but I must admit that there was probably a tear in my eye.

It was the little things that came to mind: sitting in the smelly old boot room with Taff, for example; making cups of tea; walking to the potato shop for lunch with the lads; and the Wednesday sprint training sessions. Then I walked out onto the pitch and I started to remember the roar of the crowd and some of the tries I'd scored – particularly the ten against Leeds. Then it was time to go, so I collected my boots, got into my car and left. But as I drove away I realised that I couldn't imagine going back to Central Park to play against Wigan.

7
Rugby League and Me

I've always had a love-hate relationship with Rugby League fans and the media. Some of the fans have hated me and some of the game's officials haven't been too keen on me either. On the other hand, there are those who think I am great for the game; and, in general, the media have liked me. Either way, I like to think that I've done a fair amount for the game, whatever anyone else may say.

I've been called arrogant, aloof and a show-off – but I've explained why that happens. But I think that one of the problems I've had with fans comes from the fact that they can't really identify with me. What they want to see is someone like them scoring the tries. The trouble is that I'm black, I come from London and I was educated at a boarding school in Suffolk; all the things that influenced me when I was growing up were completely different to those that influenced the majority of Rugby League players – after all, I didn't know anything about Rugby League until I was 21, by which time my personality was pretty well formed. So I'm bound to be different, and I'd never pretend to be something I'm not. I had nothing in common with most of the League fans, but I respect who they are, and I expect them to respect me for who I am.

Unfortunately I haven't always received that respect. When I signed for Wigan, for example, I made one title my own: that of the most disliked player in Rugby League. Ellery Hanley and Shaun Edwards had both been contenders for it at some stage in their careers, but even they reckoned that when I moved to Wigan I was way out on my own as the player the fans hated the most. And, of course, it's hard not to know what people think of you – and that just makes you focus more, and appear more arrogant and aloof so that it doesn't get to you.

I couldn't help noticing what was going on. Right at the beginning of my League career I remember playing for Widnes against Hull, at Naughton Park. I was feeling really full of myself after scoring a great try, and a section of the crowd starting chanting: 'Martin, Martin give us a wave.' I was a bit naïve in those days, so I turned round to wave to them – but I didn't realise that they were all Hull fans, who proceeded to give me the V-sign. My flamboyance and try-scoring celebrations make me a natural target.

Some places are worse than others, of course. I never minded going to Wigan when I was playing for Widnes, because even though the Wigan supporters were a bit one-eyed they never used to get on my back and abuse me as much as the St Helens crowd, say, or Hull supporters.

It doesn't just happen on the field, either. There have been quite a few occasions when people have had a go at me when I'm away from the pitch. Soon after the news broke that I'd been awarded an MBE, I was out with some friends in a club called 'Peruvia', in Manchester. As I walked past some bloke he said: 'Did you get an MBE?' I was looking around for a friend of mine, so I just said: 'Yeah, yeah.' He swung round and said: 'What do you mean, yeah, yeah?' I thought he was messing about, but the next thing I knew he'd taken a swipe at me. Normally I don't give people an excuse to start a fight with me: if someone comes up to me and calls me a wanker, I just say: 'OK, I'm a wanker'. But this bloke didn't even give me a chance – he just took a swing and hit me on the side of my face. He had a bottle in his other hand and tried to hit me with that – it cut my ear and ripped a brand new Armani shirt that I was wearing. Before I knew it someone else had steamed in and there was a mass brawl. Then it was suggested that I get out of there pretty quickly, and I did. To this day I hear talk about how I got beaten up in 'Peruvia'.

Thankfully there haven't been too many problems like that, because I learned how to anticipate them in the early days. I was stupid enough to go out in St Helens one night when I was playing for Widnes, but what I hadn't known was that Widnes had drawn Saints in the cup that day. So when some bloke barged into me deliberately in a club I thought: 'What's that all about?' He just stared at me, hoping for a reaction, but I didn't rise to the bait. I can just laugh things like that off, but I've been out with Paul Ince a couple of times in Manchester and no one would get away with doing that to him. Incey gets upset if people just look at him the wrong way – if I was like that I'd be fighting every night.

The whole business of fans and the relationship you have with them was completely new to me when I arrived at Widnes. I can't remember any sort of player-fan relationship when I was at Rosslyn Park – of course there were enthusiasts who watched every game, but they weren't fans in the classic sense of the word: they didn't wear a shirt with a player's name and number on it all the time; or cover a wall with pictures of their favourite players.

There was no big Alan Shearer-type welcome when I first arrived at Widnes: in fact, I turned up in Eddie McDonald's combi van – you couldn't have had a more low-key arrival. But when I ran out for my first game, and my name and number was announced, there was quite a big cheer. When a player is signed from another club all the fans know who he is, but nobody had really heard of me. Because of that, I think that the Widnes fans took to me even more when I started to do well – their feeling was: 'You're ours; we discovered you.' The fact that Widnes was such a small place heightened the effect. I thought it was great.

After a while, people started to recognise me in the street, which was weird – it was fame, albeit on a small scale. Fans would come up and ask for my autograph when I was just doing ordinary things, like shopping or sitting in a pub. I'd be interrupted by people wanting to talk to me, too, which was a new experience for me. But I did think it was a bit weird when people started looking through the windows of my house. I think that the first time I signed more than two autographs at a time was at the Hong Kong Sevens, which was a big international event, but what was happening at Widnes wasn't part of an event but was infringing on my everyday life, and I started to feel the pressure. It wasn't too bad when we were winning and I was playing well, but when we lost the mood changed, and people started to criticise me.

Of course I didn't endear myself to opposition fans. The fact that I was scoring lots of tries, hurting their team and being exuberant on the pitch meant that I was a natural target. Being taunted by fans – it happened at Warrington, St Helens and Hull in particular – was all part of playing away, and it never got me down; in fact, I used to thrive on it, because it meant that things were going well. But when I first started playing Rugby League, it was nothing out of the ordinary to go to grounds and be racially abused: I'd hear monkey chants and racial taunts from a large section of the crowd. But it used to have the opposite effect to the one that was intended, because it just spurred me on. I used to think that if I could score a hat trick I'd keep them quiet – but you can't score a hat trick every week, of course.

I was surprised, really, because there have been black players at top level in Rugby League for a lot longer than in many other sports. For example, Clive Sullivan, the former Hull wing of the late 1960s and early 1970s, was the first black sportsman to lead a British side, and, of course, Ellery Hanley has captained Great Britain on numerous occasions. It's odd that Hull should have been one of the worst grounds for racial abuse, given that one of their greatest ever players was black – they even named a road, 'Clive Sullivan Way', after him – and his son, Anthony, used to play in the city. The abuse didn't really bother me, but it's probably one of the reasons why I've never encouraged my family to come and watch me play. I'm used to abuse from fans, but I don't see why my mother should have to put up with it. But I believe things have improved and it has become less acceptable to abuse players racially now. I was happy to help change things through my involvement in a campaign to kick racism out of Rugby League.

My relationship with the Widnes fans changed completely

when it became known that I wanted to leave the club. Widnes won the First Division championship in my first two seasons there, but Wigan, our big rivals, had just begun their amazing Challenge Cup run and were beginning to dominate the game. They had a host of great players, but the Widnes fans always used to say: 'We've got the best winger in the league.' So when it became known that I wanted to leave the club, the Widnes fans seemed to take it personally – it was as though I was saying that I didn't want to be with them any more.

Once I signed for Wigan, things really turned sour and living in Widnes became unbearable. I think I stayed there for a year after I'd joined Wigan, and during that time I became a figure of hate for some of the fans. It got to the stage where I couldn't go shopping in the town because I'd be too worried that I was going to meet someone who was going to spit or swear at me: people would often call me names as I was walking past, or just start shouting at me.

Once I spotted Bobbie Goulding, the St Helens scrum-half, when I was driving through Widnes; he was driving in the opposite direction to me. We both stopped and got out of our cars for a chat, but the next minute a hail of stones came in our direction and we had to dive back into our cars and drive off. On another occasion I went shopping and ended up being followed by a gang of eight-year-olds, who all started abusing me. I didn't do anything about it for fear that I'd end up in court – but it's a bit embarrassing walking around with a gang of kids shouting at you and being powerless to do anything.

My car was often vandalised, too, and things were thrown through my windows at home and shoved through my letter box. Then people started knocking on my door at night and shouting as they walked past my house – it wasn't just kids doing it, but people of all ages. That's when I realised how fickle supporters can be. But I was worried that moving house to Wigan might be a case of 'out of the frying pan and into the fire'; I knew that everything was on a much bigger scale there, and that even if things were going well for me it would be hard to go shopping and live a normal life. So in the end I decided to live in Manchester.

I never really won over the Wigan fans despite my successes at the club. Some sections of the crowd were never convinced about me, even after my ten tries against Leeds. But then only Andy Gregory and Ellery Hanley managed to get the full backing of all the Wigan supporters. I suppose I was a victim of my own success. I was always in the papers or on television, and some people began to think, 'He's not that great, why do I keep hearing his name all the time?' I think a high profile does breed a degree of resentment. But I don't hate anybody – and if the fans hate me, that's their problem. And I didn't see too many supporting fans not cheering when I scored a try.

Of course there were rivalries on the field, as well as off it. When I first started, I think the well-established players were a bit scared of me, because I was the new kid on the block. I was the new sensation, and they set out to teach me a lesson. But it was the same when I got to the top; some people still tried to have a go at me, probably because they wanted to be where they thought I was. It never bothered me, because I've always believed that when it gets to the stage that I go round bashing young upstarts I'll know I've lost it, and it'll be time to quit the game. I also think that getting involved in the rough stuff is a diversion from what you should be trying to do in the game, and I put some of my success down to the fact that I've always focused on the way I play, and have never allowed myself to be distracted.

I'm sure that my image and flamboyant style on the pitch makes some players say, 'Give that so-and-so one for me', but I never really resented that sort of thing as it always lent a bit of spice to the game. You can't help overstepping the mark sometimes when you're wound-up about a game, but I can count the number of fights I've been involved in on one hand. And I've never really held a grievance against anyone who's done something to me on the pitch.

Back in 1989, Brian Smith, who was the Hull coach at the time, criticised me after one performance when I'd been a bit flamboyant, saying 'We can do without that in our game.' But it wasn't as if I'd hit anyone, I was just being my natural self and it didn't stop him signing me to play for St George, in Australia, when he went on to coach them. And Mike Stephenson, one of the presenters on Sky Sports, has had a go at me from time to time because of my antics. Yet whenever anyone gives me a right crack, or kicks me in the head, people say: 'It's all part of the game.' I've always had problems coming to terms with double standards like these.

I haven't had too much racial abuse from players over the years, though there's been a certain amount of general verbal abuse – but it's never been a major problem. Players sometimes say things as a reaction to a situation, but generally the intimidation is physical, with a bit of pushing and shoving, rather than verbal. I've never been sent off in my career, but I have been sin-binned a couple of times – for ridiculous reasons on both occasions. The first time it happened was when I was playing for Widnes against Hull Kingston Rovers, and a fight broke out. A player ran over to me and tried to punch me, so I ducked and pushed him away, but the referee obviously couldn't see what happened so he sent me to the sin bin. The second time I was sin-binned was after I was punched in the face by Gary Lord, of Oldham – I couldn't understand that one, and to this day it puzzles me.

Alan Hunte and Richie Eyres are both players who have been involved in well-publicised incidents with me on the pitch. Alan Hunte once head-butted me during a match at St Helens; and Richie Eyres was sent off for a high tackle on me when he was playing for Widnes in the Challenge Cup final, at Wembley in 1993. He was pretty pissed off after the game and I remember him spitting at the Wigan team bus when I was on it. But it's not as if he was sent off for something he didn't do: it was a blatant high tackle that really hurt me. The incident left me groggy and I had a headache for the rest of the game. I don't bear a grudge against either player for what happened on the pitch, but the one thing that really got to me was that they stole my filofax. It went missing when we were on the coach coming back from Swansea, where we'd been playing for England. I knew that they'd taken it but they never owned up to it – and that filofax had my whole life in it. I just couldn't understand how anyone could do something like that. However, I've spoken to Richie Eyres and Alan Hunte since then and the incident's been forgotten. I don't want to go to my grave hating anybody.

Rugby League has changed immeasurably over the ten years that I've been involved in the game, and I'd like to think that

I've played my part in improving its image and profile, although I think few people in the game would give me any kind of credit for it. To this day I think that I'm more highly thought of outside the sport than inside it – it's a shame, but I suppose that's life. If you talk to the die-hards who watch Rugby League week in week out, you'd probably find that I wasn't on their list of all-time great players; but if you asked those who followed the game in a more general sense to name the greatest players they'd seen, I would be one of the few they could actually remember.

One of the ways in which I've helped to give Rugby League a bit of a different image is through all the media attention that I've attracted. I think that the fact that I'm a black kid from Hackney who went North and made good in the game is news in itself, but the coverage I've had has been resented by some of the League fans, who see me as someone from 'down South', even though I've played the game for ten years.

Once the papers started writing about me, when I was scoring tries regularly, a certain momentum began to build up, and people began to come and see what all the fuss was about. Then the nickname 'Chariots' caught on, and there was a big debate in the Rugby League press about how good I was. It seemed that everyone had an opinion – but at least it stirred things up and created headlines that increased interest in the game. I think that the first in-depth piece about me appeared in *The Voice*, a black newspaper that wouldn't usually have carried articles about League. So from the outset I was getting the game noticed outside the normal media channels.

And the fact that I was doing well increased the amount of coverage I got. In fact, I was surprised how well things went for me – I wouldn't say it was easy, but it could have been a lot harder. It was much tougher for the likes of Jonathan Davies, who came to Rugby League with a huge reputation in Rugby Union, though I suppose I had the same problem when I started to play Union again. But I won so many things in those first few years: I was given the 'Man of Steel' award in 1988 which is the Rugby Football League's official award for the player who has had most impact during the season; I was the leading try scorer in my first four seasons; and I broke the record for notching up 100 tries in just two seasons.

Nevertheless, a lot of people didn't like the way I went about things and all the hype that came with it. Alex Murphy used to have a column in the *Daily Mirror* and he often had a go at me early in my career – he wrote some particularly nasty things when there was a debate about whether I could really play or not. I remember once speaking up for myself, and he wrote: 'Martin talks as if he's been playing the game for ten years, but he's only been playing it for five minutes. Who does he think he is?' I thought that was wrong. He was a great player in his day, but he'd become a dinosaur.

Thank God I've only had to play under him as coach once in my life – it was for Lancashire against Papua New Guinea in my first year in the game. He didn't do much then, apart from come on the pitch and rant and rave when we were playing touch rugby. But the game's become more scientific: it's more about specifics, such as ensuring that you complete your sets-of-six. Inspired speeches may get you through a game, but they're not going to make you into a championship side. I found it ironic that he slagged off Australian coaches in the past, yet when he went to Warrington as their football manager he had to work with two of them: John Dorahy and Darryl Van de Velde. I don't know how he could look Darryl in the eye after some of the things he'd written about him. I couldn't play under someone who was so two-faced.

I prefer to stay out of the limelight before big games, as I've said, but I know that you can't suddenly use the media to suit yourself, so you've just got to accept the attention. But people who have criticised me for my high media profile should take a hard look at the facts. Rugby League has always been a great game that's respected by other sportsmen, and whenever people from outside the game go to see it live they are always impressed. But how is it that so few of the players become household names? Eddie Hemmings and Mike Stephenson are two of the most well-known characters in Rugby League, yet they are commentators for Sky Sports – I think that's an indictment of the sport. I've nothing at all against them, but it can't be right that the only two people you see in the foreground when Super League is being advertised are the commentators – in 1996, at the launch of the competition, the players were only seen as a backdrop to them. Even Maurice Lindsay is a servant of the game, as are the coaches who prepare the teams and the directors who spend the money. I think that they should all be in the background and that the players should take centre stage, because that would help to push the sport – after all, it's the players that the spectators go to see.

So I make no apology for promoting myself, because whatever I've done – whether on television, in a magazine or in a poster campaign for Nike – it's always said, 'Martin Offiah, Rugby League player', so the sport has been getting publicity. (I'll get off my soapbox now.) Even to this day, a lot of people know who I am and don't know much about Rugby League – but they know I'm a Rugby League player. And there are far too few of us. Take the case of Wes Cotton, a young winger at Wigan who came down to the London Broncos. Before Wes had played a single first team game he did a bit of modelling. Suddenly he was on the front cover of two Sunday magazines and voted 'Bachelor of the Year' by *Company* magazine. In London he's more famous than Paul Newlove. Yet Paul is one of the greatest Rugby League players this country has produced, and one of the top centres in world rugby – if you ask anyone outside the North who he is, they'll say, 'Paul who?' Nothing against Wes, but I just don't understand how someone can come along and within five minutes become better known nationally than one of the best players in the sport – it would never happen in soccer, or in any other major sport. In Rugby League, people are too busy slapping themselves on the back to actually turn round, look into the outside world and see what's going on. It's no use saying: 'We've got the greatest game in the world,' and just keeping it inside the M62 corridor. You've got to go to Sheffield, Paris, London and other big cities – Newcastle, for example – and let the game stand up and be counted.

At least Super League is attracting interest and bringing the game to a wider audience. But when it was launched one of the big questions that was asked was what would happen in five years time when the Rupert Murdoch deal came to an end. The fear was that he would take his money elsewhere if Super League hadn't been successful, and the sport would be left high and dry. That's such a negative way of thinking it's untrue. I think that Super League is a wonderful opportunity for the game – and if it's as great as people say, the sport has nothing to lose. Personally, I don't think that Rupert Murdoch will pull out, particularly with people like Richard Branson becoming involved. Rugby League was very inward looking and Maurice Lindsay has done so much for the game because he looked out and saw what had to be done to capture audiences, and realised that the game had to become bigger. You have to drag some people kicking and screaming to that realisation.

When I started off in Rugby League I needed a role model, and Ellery Hanley provided it. I looked up to him, wanted to be like him, and wanted what he had. Now that I've been around a long time and achieved what I have, young people can look to me. They can see how much you can achieve through playing the game, and try to emulate me, because it's important to have role models. Jason Robinson treated me in the same way that I'd treated Ellery when he came into the game. He thought: 'Martin drives a Mercedes, so I want one; Martin's got a Nike contract, so I want one; and so on.' I took it all as a compliment. Even so, the best advice that I can give to young players is: 'Don't worry about getting a flash car. Just worry about being the best rugby player you can be and everything else will fall into place.'

I've always passed on one of the most important bits of advice that Ellery gave me on to the younger players. I emphasise that rugby's not a charity but a professional sport. I tell them, 'We're all great blokes, but we're not here because of that. We're here because we're good players and we should never lose sight of that – as soon as you stop being a good player you'll be shown the door.' In the past, players weren't that smart when it came to investing in the future but I've always encouraged everyone to get a pension and to think about getting an agent.

I think I was one of the first Rugby League players to have an agent. Ellery had a friend, John Fitzpatrick, who used to manage a lot of his business affairs, but Alan McColm was the first agent to become generally known in the game. Alan Tait introduced me to him in 1988, when I was at Widnes and things were starting to happen for me, but I didn't know how to go about getting sponsorship deals. Until then, agents weren't really needed in Rugby League, and for some time afterwards they were considered a luxury. But now agents are a necessity, as they are in most top-line sports. Players in both codes of rugby are earning six-figure sums these days so it's important to get good advice. It's hard to sell yourself but easier for someone else to do it. You do have to be careful, though, because there are a lot of unscrupulous people about. Alan's pretty well-known now, and I've recommended him to other people, but to this day there isn't a contract between us: there's only ever been a word-of-mouth agreement. Obviously we've had our disagreements, and if Alan wanted to rip me off he could, but there's a lot of trust between us and over the years we've become friends. He's Shaun's agent, and acted for Jason Robinson for a while, and now he's looking after Tulsen Tollett at the London Broncos. If something needs sorting out, or if I'm having a bad time, I'll ring Alan – because that's what he's there for, and I can just concentrate on playing. We'll probably stay together after I retire.

I've always tried to be honest, and I realise that my relationship with the sport is a two-way thing. People have thought that I'm just out for myself and what I can get, but I've never been ashamed of looking out for my own interests. I've always known that I would want to do something else at the end of my playing career, and that by making a name for myself I'd be creating an asset for when I retire. But at the same time, everything I've done has helped push the profile of the game.

8
Who Wants a Cap?

I do. I'd first decided that I wanted an England cap during that walk in Stoke Newington, when I was 15.

Playing for your country at international level represents the peak of any sportman's career. Most people think of me as a Rugby League international, but, in fact, I have a Union cap – though it's at student level, so I've tended not to talk about it much when I've been surrounded by full Union internationals at my League clubs.

The selectors noticed me while I was playing for London Division, in the Divisional Championships in December 1986, and towards the end of the 1986/87 season I was invited to go on an England Students mini-tour to France – apart from Victor Ubogu, I can't remember who else was in the squad. We played two games: the first against a French club side, in which I scored a try; and the second against the French Students.

It was my first taste of international rugby, and it seemed a lot faster than the rugby I'd been used to at home, but I was happy to get my foot on the first rung of the ladder that I hoped would lead to a full England cap. There was definitely something very special about wearing a jersey with the red rose on its chest and standing there while the national anthem was playing. But I was to be back in France sooner than I thought.

I went to League a few months later, and in January I was selected to play for Great Britain. I was surprised to win a cap so quickly, but it wasn't completely unexpected because things had gone so well for me at Widnes. I'd played against the Papua New Guinea side for Lancashire, then I had been picked for a Chairman's XIII – which was virtually a Test Trial – against Auckland and I'd scored a try. There had been talk in the press as well, with speculation that I might be selected for the game against France. And I was reasonably hopeful, too: I'd looked at the Great Britain side that had played against Papua New Guinea in October, and thought that international honours certainly weren't beyond me, but I realised it was still early days. So while I'd have been disappointed not to have been included for the match against France, I wouldn't have been devastated.

I had also realised that the League selectors went about things completely differently to their Union counterparts. Picking a Union international team seems to involve so many factors – it's not just how good you are. I suppose that one of the problems in Union is that the selectors have such a large number of players from which to choose: for example, England could pick two sides of virtually equal strength and either of them would do well in the Five Nations. And a lot depends on what type of game the coach wants to play: if he decides on a fluent, mobile style he will pick fast, ball-handling forwards, like Leicester's Neil Back; but if he wants a more static, forward-oriented game he'll choose large ball-winning forwards who can dominate the set pieces and half-backs who can kick for position. Some selections are baffling, because the players in form aren't always chosen and it makes you wonder what's going on. England's refusal to pick Jeremy Guscott during the 1997 season is a case in point.

But selection for Rugby League internationals seems much more straightforward. Of course, injuries can play a part, and sometimes you can have two really good players vying for one position, like Shaun Edwards and Bobbie Goulding, but generally the international side picks itself. I'm sure that if you asked a cross-section of supporters at the various clubs to select the Great Britain team, they would choose the same nucleus of the side as the selectors – if they were really honest and unbiased, that is. Players seem to be selected purely on merit, and there's no real consideration given to the style of play because League is a much simpler game than union.

So I made my international debut against France at Avignon, on 24 January 1988. We won fairly comfortably, by 28–14, and I scored a try by following up Shaun Edwards' chip over the French defence, gathering it and sprinting for the line. As you can imagine, I felt pretty pleased with myself – so it came as a bit of a shock when I was dropped for the return fixture at Headingley, two weeks later.

I was confused, because I thought I had done reasonably well. But, though I've never thought that coaches had a duty to explain why they were dropping you, I was relieved when Mal Reilly, the Great Britain Coach, said during an interview that I hadn't been dropped – that he just wanted to take a look at some other players. An important tour to Australia was coming up at the end of the season, so there was some logic to what he was saying, but I was still a bit worried. I knew that there had been players who had been capped against France but had never been selected again, and I wondered if I was going to share their fate. As it turned out, David Plange, the Hull Kingston Rovers' wing, took my place against France at Leeds and scored a try in the game – but he was never picked for Great Britain again.

My worries proved to be unfounded, and I was selected for the tour. It was to take in internationals against Papua New Guinea and New Zealand as well as a three-Test series against Australia: it was a tough assignment, too, because the Australians had dominated Rugby League for a long time and Great Britain hadn't won a Test against them since 1978. And I knew what to expect, because although I'd never been to Australia I'd watched quite a few Autralian club matches on video, and I was something of a fan. No one gave us much chance of winning, because we were without a number of first-choice players, including Steve Hampson, Andy Goodway and Joe Lydon. The only other Widnes player in the party, apart from me, was David Hulme.

I missed the Test against Papua New Guinea, which we won 42–22, through injury, but in the first game I played in Australia, against North Queensland, I scored four tries in our 66–16 victory. But just before the First Test against Australia, in Sydney, we lost 30–0 to Manly and the injuries began to pile up. We'd already lost Shaun Edwards who damaged his knee in Papua New Guinea and was ruled out of the rest of the tour.

We began the Test quite well, and restricted Australia to a lead of just 6–0 at half-time, but eventually we lost the match by 17–6. To be honest, I think I was out of my depth playing against Australia, because the game was so much faster and tougher than anything I'd been used to. I was certain that I'd be dropped for the Second Test, at Lang Park, but fortunately I retained my place – as a result of injuries and the fact that I played in a midweek game in Brisbane and scored a hat-trick. We played a bit better this time, and I scored quite a good try, leaving Wally Lewis, the Australian captain, trailing in my wake on the way to the line, but it was a rough, undisciplined affair and we went down by 34–14.

Another whitewash looked to be on the cards, particularly as we were picking up even more injuries: in addition to Shaun Edwards, we lost Andy Platt, Garry Schofield, Paul Medley, Lee Crooks and Paul Dixon; and the squad was so depleted that replacements had to be flown out. I was joined by my Widnes team-mates Andy Currier, Darren Wright, Richie Eyres and Paul Hulme, but the Australian press had already written us off: one journalist calling the match 'a sham'. We really had our backs to the wall and the result seemed a foregone conclusion.

In the event, everything just went right for us that day in Sydney. We all played out of our skins: Andy Gregory was fantastic; Phil Ford, who was playing full-back, scored a really great try; and I managed to score another, to give us a 10–0 lead at half-time. Australia hit back after the interval, but two tries from Henderson Gill kept us in front and the match was sealed by a score from Mike Gregory, who was playing second-row, that has become a classic: he made a break from his own half and I tried to get with him but was held back by Wally Lewis; I didn't think Mike would make it, but he was determined to go all the way on his own – he did it, and the try has become a classic in the history of Rugby League. It was an historic win, and in twenty or thirty years' time I'm sure it will be seen as a watershed for Rugby League Tests between Great Britain and Australia, because it showed that the Aussies weren't invincible.

There's a different level of intensity in the game when you play the Australians, and I found that the only thing to do was to just throw myself into the action and hope and pray that I would come out on the other side: you couldn't look too far ahead, just to the next tackle. But I enjoyed playing in Australia, because Rugby League is the number one sport in Queensland and New South Wales, and is especially popular in Sydney, so I was in my element. Even so, there have been quite a few times when playing against Australian sides when we didn't think we had a hope in hell of winning. But the fear of embarrassment makes you try even harder, and when you've got that 'backs-to-the-wall' attitude, you never know what can happen. That was how we felt when Widnes took on the Canberra Raiders, in the World Club Challenge at Old Trafford, in 1989; when Great Britain played Australia in Melbourne; in 1992; and when Wigan confronted the Broncos in Brisbane in 1994.

It doesn't always work out like that, of course. A lot of people were optimistic that we would win a series against the Australians for the first time since 1970 when they toured Britain in 1990. The opening Test was played at Wembley – it was my first appearance there, and the first time I'd played in London since turning professional. And it turned out to be a great day in another way, because we won and I scored a try. It wasn't one of my more spectacular efforts, though: Ellery Hanley chipped the ball through to Gary Belcher, their full-back, and went through to challenge him; I followed up, picked the ball up on the half-volley and beat Andrew Ettingshausen to the touchdown. We won by 19–12, and after the game we really believed that we could win the series.

The next Test was played at Old Trafford. It was a tough game, but we had a good first half. Then I damaged my knee ligaments just after the interval, when Mal Meninga, the Australian captain, fell on me and I had to go off – I watched the rest of the game on a monitor in the treatment room, with ice packs on my knee.

We had been promised a £3,500 win-bonus, and with a minute to go it seemed that there was a good chance that we would collect it, because we had the Australians on the defensive, deep inside their own 22. But suddenly Ricky Stuart, their scrum-half, spotted a gap and broke away and passed to Meninga – who ran all the way down the touchline to score the try that gave them victory and levelled the series. I just had to sit there and watch as he ran away to score: all I was thinking about was that if I'd been on the pitch instead of the treatment table I would have been able to catch him and prevent the try – then we would probably have won the Test and the series and changed the history of Rugby League. Of course, I might have fallen over or missed a tackle – but you don't think of things like that. I didn't play again until the Third Test, at Elland Road, Leeds, but it rained throughout the match and I didn't really get much of a chance to do anything. The Australians showed real commitment and professionalism to win the game by 14–0, and with it the series.

My next encounter with Australia came on the 1992 tour. After just two minutes of the First Test, at the Sydney Football

Stadium, I was put away and beat Allan Langer, the Australian scrum-half, before going past Andrew Ettingshausen – but I was called back because the touch judge said that I'd put my foot in touch. Twenty minutes later I was put away again, and this time Ettingshausen managed to force me into touch again. If I'd have scored on either of those occasions it might have turned the game – on the first occasion it was probably only a matter of a millimetre of chalk – but the Australians came back strongly to beat us by 22–6.

The Second Test was played in Melbourne in typically British weather – persistent rain – and we responded with a terrific performance. We were 22–0 up at half-time, and although they came back at us in the second half I managed to score one myself from a pass by Garry Schofield. Our 33–10 win equalled the highest ever for a Great Britain side against Australia and set us up for the series decider in Brisbane. But it was to be the same old story: we just couldn't string two Test wins together. It was another tough game, but the Australians were simply too strong for us and, although the try I scored late in the game from a kick ahead kept our hopes alive, we were well and truly beaten.

Later in the year we had the chance to make amends at Wembley when we faced Australia in the 1992 World Cup Final, in October. This was the game that was promoted with a poster campaign with the slogan: 'Will the Australians catch Offiah at Wembley?', so I had a lot to live up to. In fact, I shouldn't really have been playing, because I was carrying a chronic hamstring injury and I wasn't really fit. The game was really tight, and I felt I had to do something to justify all the hype, but I just didn't get any chances. We led 6–4 going into the second half, thanks to the goal kicking of Deryck Fox, but a mistake by Alan Hunte and a missed tackle by John Devereux allowed Steve Renouf, the Australian centre, to score and we lost by 10–6.

I was so disappointed that we'd lost and that I hadn't got into the game at all, especially after the poster campaign, that I didn't feel like hanging around, so instead of walking around the pitch I just headed for the dressing room. Shaun and Ellery were going to walk off with me, but as I went a section of the crowd started booing, and suddenly the whole stadium seemed to be booing me. Sensibly, Shaun and Ellery stayed on the pitch.

The newspapers were full of stories saying that I was a bad sportsman after the incident, but there was nothing to say that we had to go on a lap of honour if we lost. If we'd won, I wouldn't have been concerned whether or not the losing team did a lap of honour. I think that it's for the victors to enjoy the spoils, and for the vanquished to leave the field to them. But I've never been a good loser. I can remember playing for a cardboard cup covered in silver paper in a primary-school football competition: my team lost in the final and Chike took the mickey out of me, so I chased after him, fell over and scraped my knee. And I don't think it's good to get into the habit of losing and not be concerned about it, because you start to accept losing – and that's no good at all.

But perhaps we made amends for the 1992 defeat two years later, when we returned to Wembley for the First Test of the 1994 series against Australia. The game was a classic: it was the one in which Shaun Edwards was sent off early for a high tackle on Bradley Clyde, the Australian loose-forward. We were down to 12 men and really up against it, but the whole team put in a fantastic effort defensively and made so many tackles that we stayed in the game. Jason Robinson and I worked really hard, running from dummy-half to make valuable yards and give our forwards a breather. The game was really close until Jonathan Davies exploded into the line, broke through and raced to the corner for one of the best tries ever seen at Wembley. We won 8–4, and suddenly everyone was thinking: 'If we can beat Australia with twelve men, what can we do with thirteen?' But it never really works out like that, of course. Yet again we couldn't put two consecutive wins together, and we were hammered 38–8 in the Second Test, then beaten 23–4 in the Third, at Elland Road. And although I've achieved a lot in my career, it's really disappointing that I haven't managed to win a Test series against Australia.

I've been more successful against New Zealand, though my games against the Kiwis have not been without incident. The first match I played against them was in 1988, when we were scheduled to play one Test in Christchurch after our tour of Australia. We lost 12–10, but the only thing that I can remember about the game was the weather. I don't think I've ever been as cold in my life.

In 1989, New Zealand came to Britain and I played in all three Tests. The Kiwis weren't considered to be as strong a side as Australia, but we got a shock in the First Test, at Old Trafford, when they beat us 24–16. At least I had the satisfaction of scoring one of the best tries of my career in that game: I picked the ball up on my own 22-metre line and ended up scoring under the posts. The Second Test at Elland Road didn't start well for Great Britain, because Steve Hampson, our full-back, was sent off after only two minutes for butting Gary Freeman, the New Zealand scrum-half. But despite playing with only 12 men for most of the game we won 26–6, which was a fantastic achievement, and I collected another try thanks to a pass from Shaun Edwards. The final Test at Wigan was a much closer affair: I scored a try early on, after a break from Shaun Edwards, and almost got another one, after a long kick and chase, but was eventually denied by the fingertips of Kelly Shelford. The match ended 10–6 in our favour, and I got the man-of-the-match award, which they said was for my defensive effort, and I became the only player to score a try in all three Tests against New Zealand.

There was a tour to Papua New Guinea and New Zealand in the summer of 1990, but I missed the first part of it because I needed an operation on a toe injury so I flew out to meet the rest of the party in New Zealand. We didn't go into the First Test in particularly good spirits, because we'd just been beaten 24–13 by Auckland, and it proved to be another tough, tight affair. But going into the second half we were leading 11–10, thanks to a drop goal from Garry Schofield. Then I intercepted the ball when the Kiwis were attacking our line, midway through the half, and raced up the other end – I thought that I'd wrapped up the match, but the referee ruled that I was offside. But our defence held in a pretty tense final quarter, and we ended up winning by the single point.

I hadn't scored in any of the three games I'd played, and I think that some of the critics were questioning whether it had been worth flying me out to join the tour. But I answered them when it looked as if we'd blown the Second Test, at Auckland, because we were losing 14–12 with a few minutes remaining.

The message came out from the bench to attack from anywhere, so Kelvin Skerrett launched himself from our 22. Then Garry Schofield and Darryl Powell took play to the halfway line, and the ball was worked out to me on the left wing. The final pass wasn't a particularly good one, because it was a bit behind me, and I had to take it with one hand, and Kevin Iro was breathing down my neck. I just took off and sprinted up the touchline to score – it proved to be the try that won the match and clinched the series.

But just to prove how cruel fate can be, I made my worst ever blunder in the very next Test. A few minutes into the game, Bobbie Goulding broke through, and as he had a New Zealand player chasing him, he passed the ball to me to make sure of the try. I went behind the posts, and I was just about to put the ball down when I stumbled slightly and it popped out of my grasp. It was just one of those things, but because we lost the match 21–18 I got the blame – even though I did score a try later on. I got a lot of stick for that mistake, and was reminded of it for years afterwards. It even featured in a commercial on New Zealand television: the idea was the same as in the Hamlet cigar advertisements, where something always goes horribly wrong, except that in the New Zealand versions they were advertising something called 'Minties'. I believe the ad was quite popular out there – certainly all the Kiwi players would remind me about it whenever they saw me.

My last international appearance was for England against France at Gateshead, in June 1996, when I scored four tries. But I can't complain, because I've had a pretty good international career playing for Great Britain. And my record's not bad: I've scored 26 tries in 33 Tests.

I enjoyed playing international football, because I relished the challenge of taking a step up from club rugby, and it was interesting to meet different players and coaches and work with them. Mal Reilly was the first coach I played under for Great Britain: he ruled by fear, not so much because he ranted or raved but because he commanded respect. He trained hard, and looked fit enough to play – in fact, on the 1988 tour he was probably fitter than a lot of the squad. He had been a great player, and everyone was aware of his reputation, so when he said something everyone really sat up and took notice. Mal could also inspire you, and our victory against Australia in the Third Test in Sydney was probably a testimony to his motivational powers.

He was quite a hard taskmaster on tour, making us train twice a day, and he hardly used to give us any time off. If we were given more than one or two days to ourselves during the whole tour we were very lucky. On one occasion the players had a meeting and decided we wanted a day off. But the big question was, 'Who's going to ask Mal?' We had some great players in that party – men like Ellery Hanley, Andy Platt, Kevin Ward and Andy Gregory who had all been around a long time and were well-respected – but they were all too scared to ask him for a day off. I thought that was pretty incredible.

Ellery Hanley took over from Mal for the 1994 series against Australia, and it was really weird. It didn't really sit well with me, because he was still a good friend of mine and I didn't know whether to take him seriously – he'd always been the biggest joker around and had always messed about in training. We'd used to try to make each other laugh during Great Britain squad sessions, and often ended up in trouble. It's difficult to have a relationship like that with someone one day and have him as the boss the next. But Ellery had in his favour the fact that he was a great player, and everyone knew that he wouldn't ask you to do something he wouldn't have done himself. In fact, he was good enough and fit enough to play against Australia in the 1994 series, and it would probably have been better if he had, because the squad was weakened by injuries and we ended up having to play Phil Clarke, who was normally a loose-forward, at stand-off in the Third Test.

After Ellery left to play in Australia, Phil Larder took over as Great Britain Coach – he had always been around on the international scene, and had been part of the coaching team when Mal Reilly was in charge. He couldn't inspire players in the same way as Mal, but he was a great thinker and student of the game. Whenever you had a conversation with him he'd pick your brains and listen to what you said.

I got on well with all the Great Britain coaches, and always found it easy to talk to them. It was great to meet all the Wigan players when I first started playing international rugby. Being in the same team as Shaun, Ellery and Andy Goodway gave me a real buzz – and when I eventually joined Wigan, playing for Great Britain felt like playing at Central Park, because so many of the Wigan players were in the Great Britain squad.

I've been to Australia about eight times – I even flew there twice in 1992 – and I've always enjoyed touring, but the fact is that I hate flying. I've got a real phobia about it. I've learned to control my fear as I've grown older, but if I can avoid flying I will. I used to look at the tour itinerary and work out the number of flights we would be taking. On the first one, in

1988, there were more than 20, and I really wasn't looking forward to it. I even began to think of ways of getting out of the tour, but I said to myself, 'If you don't go and the plane doesn't crash, you're going to really regret it.' So I decided that I couldn't let my phobia interfere with my life. Even so, sometimes I've been quite grateful to be injured because I haven't had to fly to a game; but if it's been an important tour match I've always got on the plane. Paul Newlove has the same problem, I know – we've roomed together a couple of times and talked about it – and he's let it interfere with his career to a certain extent by pulling out of trips.

Once the plane gets up in the air I don't feel too bad if it's not too bumpy, but it's always on my mind that anything could happen. I think I must be a bit of a control freak, because whenever I'm not in control of something in my life I become very cautious – I suppose it's part of my psychological make-up. I used to take sleeping tablets and air sickness pills to help me get through the flight, and on one flight to Australia I took so many that I don't even remember getting off the plane at the stop-over, in Singapore. And one of the few times I would ever drink in the early days was when we were flying: in 1991, when I was flying out to play for St George, in Sydney, I got so zonked out that I went to sleep and woke up in Sydney – it was the best plane journey I've every had! The scariest time I've had was in 1988, when I was in a small light aircraft flying to Canberra from Sydney. It was going up and down so much I was desperate to get off, and I never thought I'd live to tell the tale.

Despite my fear of flying, I've enjoyed most of the tours I've been on. But I came close to being sent home from the 1990 tour to New Zealand, thanks to Bobbie Goulding. It was when

I'd just joined the tour party, having flown in late after minor surgery on my injured toe. We were given the rest of the day off after a training session, but the place we were in was really boring: there was nothing to do. So I got into a silly drinking game with Bobbie Goulding and some others. I got very drunk, and when I went to the toilet Bobbie followed me and ended up smashing the door into my foot. He insisted on giving me a piggy-back ride, and as we were charging around the hotel we came across Mal Reilly and Phil Larder, who were having dinner. The next day my foot was so sore that I couldn't train, which didn't please the management. I think that they thought about sending me home, but, thankfully, they didn't. I was none too popular – but I managed to score the winning try in the Second Test, which won us the series.

One of the main reasons for changing codes was that I wanted to try to fulfil my ambition of winning a Rugby Union cap. When I played at Twickenham, for Wigan against Bath, I thought: 'I wouldn't mind playing here when it's full'. I reckoned that if I got the chance to go back there in an England shirt I might be able to treat the crowd to something special. Before I switched codes there was talk that the England management would take a look at me at the Middlesex Sevens, but I had some bad press on my return to Union because I missed Bedford's early games through injury. And there are differences between playing on the wing in League and Union – the lines of running to get yourself into the game are different, for example – and it took me some time to adjust.

Alan Tait, my old Widnes team-mate, has shown it's not impossible to make the switch successfully. When he joined

Newcastle and returned to Union, in 1996, Alan wasn't a League international – in fact, he couldn't even get into the Leeds team. But he ended up playing for Scotland in the Five Nations, and going on the Lions tour to South Africa. John Bentley made the Lions tour, too, while Jim Fallon, the former Leeds wing, got into the England squad following his return to Union with Richmond. I think that it's a testament to Rugby League that they could all achieve so much when they hadn't played Union for such a long time.

I played against John Bentley last season in Bedford's first match against Newcastle. They beat us quite convincingly, and he scored an interception try. But when he was interviewed after the game, he said that when he'd played against me in Rugby League I'd always been on the better team – it seemed to me as though he was saying that the only reason I had been successful was that I had been in good teams. I was a bit insulted, because I felt that he had tried to belittle my achievements. Normally I don't take these things personally, but I must admit that I was more fired up than usual before the return match, at Goldington Road. I thought that if we beat them while I was playing for Bedford his theory would be demolished. And I had a pretty good game that day – and was lucky enough to score the winning try, so I was well pleased.

9
The Super League Revolution

The advent of Super League really was revolutionary. It brought with it the biggest changes that the game had seen since it came into existence, over a hundred years ago. It's origins were in Australia, and a battle there between the media moguls Kerry Packer and Rupert Murdoch for control of Rugby League in the country.

Kerry Packer had bought the television rights to Australian Rugby League (ARL) games – the ARL controlled League in Queensland and New South Wales, where it is the largest sport – for his Channel Nine. This effectively denied Rupert Murdoch's television interests access to the game, so Murdoch set about creating his own competition: he called it 'Super League', and signed up a whole host of top players, as well as some of the big clubs, such as the Brisbane Broncos, the Canberra Raiders and the Auckland Warriors. But he also had a wider vision, and created new clubs outside the New South Wales stronghold of the ARL, in places such as Adelaide, Perth and North Queensland. Murdoch's News Corporation then came up with the idea of establishing a Super League in Europe, with the eventual aim of holding international competitions between the European and Australian sides, and making Rugby League a global game.

In Britain, the Rugby Football League decided that Super League, with its ambitious plans and injection of capital, was the way forward, and in April 1995 it announced a deal with News Corporation to establish such a competition, for which it would receive £87 million over five years. 'The European Super League', as it would be called, would have just 12 teams, including several new clubs created by the merger of smaller ones, and would switch to playing rugby in the summer. Even though some people weren't too keen on summer rugby, and the mergers never actually took place, personally I felt that this was the right way for Rugby League to go. In the event, the concept was adopted.

Things weren't going as smoothly in Australia, however. Having seen many of the best players signed up for the new competition, the ARL reacted by setting their sights on the top British players. Of course, Super League couldn't allow its British clubs to be stripped of their best players, so a bidding war broke out between the ARL and Super League as the 1994/95 season was drawing to a close. Everyone wanted the big names from the British game, so the Australians came over here with fat cheque books and the result was an amazing few months.

I began to hear rumours about what was happening on the Wednesday prior to our league game against Hull, the last one of the season, but things really started to take off on Friday, when I had a telephone call from Jack Robinson, the Wigan Chairman. He asked me if I was interested in signing a new contract and taking a Super League pay off – obviously, the idea was to keep me away from the ARL.

Now although my contract with Wigan had just over 12 months to run, I had wanted to give myself a bit of time to negotiate a new one, so at the start of 1995 I'd talked to Jack Robinson about a new contract and he said he'd get back to me – but he never did. My agent, Alan McColm, was aware of the situation in Australia and we discussed the possibility that I might play there full-time until the end of my career, because Wigan hadn't responded after my initial enquiry about my contract. I didn't really want to play for any other club in England apart from Wigan, so going to Australia seemed the only other option. But the next thing that happened was that I got a phone call from Jack Robinson, who asked if I would accept a one-off Super League payment of £100,000, plus a contract with the club for £75,000 a year over the next three years.

Suddenly I'd gone from a situation in which the chairman of the club hadn't bothered to get back to me after my enquiry, to one in which I was being offered all this money. I told Jack that if he had offered me these terms three months ago, I would have probably bitten his hand off – but the situation had changed since then. As it turned out, I was sensible not to accept his first offer, because the figures, in all cases, would eventually increase by 100 per cent.

I remember going to training on the Saturday and the place was buzzing. Everybody was asking 'Are you ARL or are you Super League?' It was a very unnerving time, because all kinds of figures were being bandied around and players were off having little discussions all over the place. I don't know what it was like at other clubs, but as Wigan was the premier club, every single player was involved, from those who had only just come into the squad, like Kris Radlinski, Simon Haughton and Craig Murdock, to the top stars, such as Va'aiga Tuigamala and Jason Robinson.

It was hard to believe the amount of money that was being discussed. The ARL was reportedly offering some players four-year contracts at £250,000 a year – and £1 million to play Rugby League is a staggering amount of money. There were rumours that Gary Connolly and Jason Robinson were more likely to go with the ARL, as they eventually did, and that others, like Andy Farrell, were here, there and everywhere discussing their options. Players were asking me for advice and I didn't really know what to say.

On the Sunday of the match, things were really getting out of hand. We were playing Hull at Central Park and my head was so full of the whole business, that I actually missed the exit off the motorway on the way to the ground, and nearly ended up on the way to Cumbria. And before the game, the talk in the dressing room wasn't about how we were going to play but about contracts and what colour of Mercedes or BMW players were going to buy. They were saying, 'We're going to be on soccer players' wages', and a lot of them still didn't understand what was going on. Thankfully we still managed to win the game well, by 66–16 – don't ask me how – and I scored two tries.

On Monday I walked into the office at Wigan and the board outlined the terms of a new deal that was so good I really couldn't refuse it. So I went to the Midland Hotel, in Manchester, met the representatives of Super League and ended up signing three different contracts: a contract with Wigan, a contract for Super League, and a contract that involved promotional work for Sky Television.

Uppermost in my mind, and that of the other players, was that I couldn't afford to miss the boat, because the sums of money on offer were staggering. I signed a contract for more money than I ever imagined I'd earn, and I couldn't help but think back to when I first signed for Widnes in 1987. I thought I'd really made it when Dougie Laughton gave me a cheque for £1,000 and told me to go on holiday. So as I signed the three contracts I was thinking about how far I'd come in just eight years.

But I still couldn't believe what was happening to me – it didn't really sink in. I'd had a big offer to go and play in Australia, but at that stage in my career I wasn't really interested – I was fairly well-known in this country, but if I had gone to Australia for four years, people over here would have forgotten about me. You only had to look at what happened to Ellery Hanley: he used to be the leading name in British Rugby League, but since he left Leeds to go to Australia I've only seen his name mentioned in the press about three times in 18 months. I knew how I wanted my career to go after I finished playing rugby, and with that in mind I thought it was best to stay here in England. It would have been more beneficial for me financially to play in Australia, but you can't put a price on peace of mind and happiness. Instead of taking the extra £50,000 or £100,000 I'd rather be in Britain, and focused on what I wanted to do.

Super League representatives took steps to try and secure the entire Wigan squad. Even those who had hardly played any first team rugby were being offered new contracts, as well as a one-off payment of £30,000, before a ball had been kicked. But to be fair to the Wigan players, they didn't let it go to their heads: they still realised that the one thing they were there for was to play Rugby League, and they remained focused.

The Australian money-men went round to all the big clubs, such as St Helens and Warrington, and were particularly keen to sign young players like Keiron Cunningham, the Saints hooker. I think it was the ARL representatives rather than the Super League ones that were involved in a mad scramble, because they knew that they desperately needed players in order to run their competition. Super League had signed up most of the top Australians, like Laurie Daley and Allan Langer – who were reportedly on astronomical contracts of a million dollars a year – so it was a question of signing up as many British players as they could and deciding what they were going to do with them later. Eventually this policy blew up in their faces, because some of the players they had signed were sent back from Australia once the competition had started, because they weren't needed.

The first sign that all this new money was around at Wigan was that Jason Robinson bought a brand new BMW 328i convertible. Now I've had a few nice cars over the years and I've been in the game for a long time – yet here was this 20-year-old kid buying himself a £35,000 car. It's one thing to hear about the kind of money people are getting, but it's only when you actually see things like this you realise just what has happened.

Of course all this money may seem excessive, but sport has become big business and it's all relative: for example, an average salary for a top footballer in the Premier League is probably around £10,000–£12,000 a week, so Rugby League players are only earning today what soccer players used to earn ten years ago. But it's certainly a far cry from the old days before the contract system was introduced into Rugby League, in 1987. Then, all you received was a signing-on fee and your match payments on top of that, and these varied according to whether you won or lost. The money the players earned from the game was really just pocket money for grown-ups: it might help them buy a few things, but it didn't make any major changes to their lifestyle; certainly it wasn't possible to be a full-time player on what they earned. Reaching the Challenge Cup Final at Wembley may have earned them a bit extra, but, apart from that, I gather the only other way to get extra cash was to knock on the chairman's door every three or four months and tell him you weren't happy – maybe he'd slip you a few quid.

Thank goodness it's all changed. I've certainly got a lot to thank Rugby League for: I have a good lifestyle: I drive nice cars and I've one house in Manchester and two apartments in London. And it's all come from playing Rugby League – nothing else. Yet people tend to associate an affluent lifestyle with playing soccer, being an actor and the like; nobody really thinks of Rugby League players being in that category. In fact, a lot of people in this country still don't know what League is.

There's no doubt that Super League has really lifted the game. It has given it a lot more credibility, and I don't see that either players or supporters have any grounds for complaint: the players because they're paid so well, and the supporters because the fact that so many more players can afford to become full-time professionals has meant that standards have risen. And young players just coming into the game have also benefited, because they are offered decent contracts that put a few quid into their pockets. If their career in rugby doesn't work out, they've still got some money to show for their efforts, so they're more likely to take the plunge and see if they can make a go of the game. Together with the introduction of the Academy sides for players under 19, this has been great for the game. All the top clubs are running Academy teams, which provide young players with a good standard of competition and good coaching, all under the umbrella of a professional club.

And I think that Academy football is producing players of far higher quality than those who come through from amateur Rugby League. You're always going to get naturally gifted players, such as Andy Gregory and Shaun Edwards, who take the time to learn the skills, but we need many more of them and I believe that the Academy system is a way of finding them. It's easier for young players to graduate to the first team now, because it's not as great a jump in standard as it is from the amateur ranks. The only real difference between Academy rugby and first-team rugby is the maturity of the players – Academy players are mini-professionals.

The inaugural Super League season was excellent, too. Normally the big games in the Rugby League calendar are Wigan v St Helens, or Wigan v Leeds, but suddenly there were a number of important fixtures that didn't involve Wigan, such as St Helens v London Broncos, and Bradford Bulls v St Helens. Super League has made the game more exciting and without it, I think Wigan's domination would have continued.

In fact, there's only one problem about Super League as far as I'm concerned: despite all that Sky Sports has done for the game, I believe that Rugby League is being held back by it's lack of any real presence on terrestrial television. Sky can't take a minority sport and make it successful; what it does is to buy the rights to show sports that are already successful for a high price, and do good things with it – but that limits the sport's growth. It's hard for a game like Rugby League to expand into new areas, because its not being shown to an audience that's wide enough. The only Rugby League on national terrestrial television is the Challenge Cup, and even that has been downgraded somewhat with the advent of Super League. And I think that this lack of coverage has really hurt the game, because I believe truly national television exposure is vital.

It may have been an excellent season in general, but for me the first Super League season was very disappointing. Most of the tries that I've scored have come in good conditions. I used to get a lot at the beginning of the season and a lot at the end, when the weather tended to improve and the pitches weren't so heavy. And during the winter months I used to think that if I could keep things ticking over with a few tries I would be among the top try-scorers come the end of the season. So I was looking forward to playing Rugby League in the summer, and I scored two tries in Wigan's first game against Oldham. But in the second game, against St Helens, I cracked a bone in my back as a result of a tackle.

When I returned I did well, scoring five tries against Bath in the cross-code challenge match at Maine Road, but after injuring my toe playing for Great Britain against France, I began to struggle for fitness and following my transfer from Wigan to the London Broncos I only managed four games for them before the end of the first Super League season. So Super League was hardly a personal triumph for me. But Rugby League was never going to be the same again.

10
League vs Union

For as long as anyone can remember there have been arguments about whether League or Union has the best players, and about what would happen if a League team played a Union team. And in 1996, almost overnight, it became possible to decide the arguments one way or another, when the International Rugby Football Board, Union's controlling body, decided to allow Union to become 'open' – in other words, professionalism was now acceptable. Suddenly players could switch codes without being banned for ever from the Union game, and League and Union players could play on the same pitch.

The obvious thing to do was to pit Bath, the Union champions, against Wigan, the champions of League. But setting the games up wasn't quite as straightforward as it seemed. Both clubs had heavy commitments: Bath were still involved in the chase for league and cup honours, while Wigan were just about to embark on the inaugural Super League season. However, Alan McColm, my agent, was involved in setting up the matches, and when the clubs realised that they could make quite a bit of money out of them it was full-steam ahead. Bath probably wouldn't have agreed if it hadn't been for the fact that they realised they would need considerable finance to cope with the professional era, which was just round the corner. In the event, though, I think that they were pleased that they had accepted the challenge, because their eyes were opened to the world of professional rugby and they learned some valuable lessons.

Anyway, the decision was made eventually: there would be two games, one played under League rules at Maine Road in Manchester and another under Union laws at Twickenham. And they captured the imagination of the public to such an extent that they proved one of the sporting highlights of the year. They also did a lot to break down the barriers between the codes, and certainly helped to educate both sets of supporters. A lot of people outside Rugby League weren't aware of great players like Gary Connolly, Henry Paul, Andy Farrell and Jason Robinson so the matches brought them to a wider audience and there was a greater appreciation of their talents – not surprisingly, Gary and Jason went on to play Rugby Union for Harlequins and Bath respectively, on short-term contracts. Prior to the games against Bath, probably the only League players most Union followers knew about were Shaun Edwards and Ellery Hanley, as well the former international Union players such as Jonathan Davies and me.

I'm glad I took part in the matches because they were historic occasions and they'll be talked about for years to come – I can't see cross-code matches happening again on anything like such a grand scale. But, if nothing else, they really highlighted the fact that Union and League are two different sports.

Wigan prepared for the match under League rules in just the

same way that we'd prepare for a normal game: it took place on 8 May 1997 at Maine Road, Manchester – the home of Manchester City Football Club. It was my first game back after breaking a bone in my back against St Helens, and I really enjoyed myself in the 82–6 win, scoring five tries. If we'd played properly for 80 minutes, though, the score would have been 100–0. We only played hard for 40 minutes, and the likes of Henry Paul and Andy Farrell were substituted quite early on – in some ways I thought it was wrong for us not to try to win as comprehensively as we could, because it allowed some bigots in the Union code to hold on to a degree of comfort. It would probably have made the return game under Union laws a lot easier, too, because Bath managed to score a try and got some credit from the media, which gave them something to build on for the return game. They probably thought 'OK, you won that game easily, but we didn't give up. We were matching you towards the end, we scored a try, and you're professional athletes, anyway.' But a side that's beaten 100–0 has nothing left to hang on to at all – I know that Shaun was very upset that we didn't play to the limit for the full 80 minutes.

Before Wigan played the return game against Bath, under Union laws, we played in the Middlesex Sevens. When I first heard that we'd been invited I was amazed. There are a number of major events in the Rugby Union calendar, such as the Five Nations and the Varsity Match, and the Middlesex Sevens is one of them. I'd played there twice for Rosslyn Park, and although we'd hadn't managed to win it, I'd really enjoyed the occasion and loved playing in the tournament.

After the news had sunk in, I knew that we were going to win the competition. Sevens is a more open game than the 15-a-side version, and it's easier for teams from Rugby League to compete. And sevens is a very natural game for me, because I believe the extra space benefits fast creative players – and Wigan had a lot of these, so I knew that we'd do well. In fact, it might be an idea to have a sevens tournament every year involving League and Union teams: it would certainly make for an interesting competition. Even though both Wigan and St Helens declined to enter the Middlesex Sevens in 1997, I think it would be a good idea for a league team to be represented in the event in the future.

There are no words to describe what it felt like as I walked out onto the pitch at Twickenham for the Sevens. It was a big thrill to be there with all my mates, and we had a really good squad that included Jason Robinson, Gary Connolly and Va'aiga Tuigamala – although we were up against some strong sides in Harlequins, Wasps, Leicester and, of course, Rosslyn Park. There was quite a buzz around us: when we arrived, you could hear people saying, 'Look, there's the Rugby League team.' The supporters seemed to leave the car parks to see our games, whereas normally they just stay out there and drink for most of the afternoon. It was great, because they could actually see for themselves what the Wigan team was all about. It was a bit difficult in the changing rooms at first, though, because there was a bit of an 'us and them' situation: Rugby Union v Rugby League. I heard talk from some of the other teams along the lines of 'Just beat them, we don't want them coming down here and showing us up.' But that's more to do with professional pride, I suppose, than any inherent nastiness.

We'd done some specialist training for sevens – one of the

Orrell coaches came down to help us, and we played some games amongst ourselves – but otherwise we prepared in the same way as for a normal game of Rugby League. But we felt that there was a bit of pressure on us, because of all the media attention, and thought that we really did have to get to the final at least. Twickenham may have been a new experience for most of the Wigan lads, but they were quality players who had all played in big arenas before, and I think they were determined to do well. We knew that we had the ability to score tries, so our main priority was defence. In a lot of sevens matches a pattern develops in which one side scores and then the other replies immediately. So when we scored, we were determined to prevent our opponents from hitting back straight away. We had some trouble with our tackling, though: Gary Connolly was penalised a couple of times for tackles that would have been considered good hits in league.

We won our first game, against Richmond, comfortably by 48–5, but we had to come from behind to win in a couple of other games: we were 12 points down at one stage in our second match, against Harlequins, before we rallied to win 36–24. Then we played Leicester in the semi-final, and ran out 35–12 winners to put ourselves into the final against Wasps. They were captained by Lawrence Dallaglio, the England flanker, and their scrum-half was Andy Gomarsall, who went on to play for England. Wasps took a 15-point lead but the Wigan players showed great commitment to fight back, and eventually win the match 38–15. It wasn't easy coping with the laws, and the final against Wasps was a tough game, but all the lads were up for it – and I think our professionalism and fitness won through in the end.

I always enjoy playing sevens, but I found the tournament quite tough because I'd only recently come back from the injury to my back, so I wasn't 100 per cent fit. I was in a fair amount of pain and didn't play in the semi-final, and I went off in the final. But we had quality back-up in the shape of Kris Radlinski and Rob Smyth, and they saw us through. Of course, most of the Union followers had never heard of them, which illustrates one of Rugby League's problems: here were two outstanding youngsters that were more or less unknown; they weren't receiving the same amount of acclaim as their equivalents in Union. I think that Wigan did an enormous amount of good for Rugby League by winning the Middlesex Sevens.

Nevertheless, the whole day was a very special one for me, partly because nobody had expected us to win the tournament, but partly, also, because I'd never achieved anything like this success in my Union days with Rosslyn Park. And I saw quite a few people that I knew in the crowd, like Woolverstone Hall old-boy Cedric Carr, who also played for Rosslyn Park, as well as some other friends from school and my Union days. I was also presented with a tie by the Penguins, the side I'd played for in the Sevens in Hong Kong, in 1987. So, all in all, I felt as if I'd come back to my roots.

When we were having our pictures taken after winning the trophy, the whole team started singing, 'Working class, working class, working class', which was pretty funny. And we carried on singing on the bus on the way back to the hotel. Later we had a party in Planet Hollywood for Liverpool, who had just lost the FA Cup Final at Wembley, before ending up at the Hanover Grand, a club in the West End of London.

Wigan's win in the Sevens really set things up for the return match in the cross-code challenge, at Twickenham, under Union laws – everyone suddenly started to think that Wigan could win. We knew we weren't going to get beaten by as much as we had beaten Bath, at Maine Road, and we believed we had a chance of giving them a game. We prepared for the game by having a few sessions against Orrell, but doing so made me realise why League clubs are unlikely to want to repeat the cross-code challenges: doing the job properly takes a fair degree of application, and going up to Orrell for training sessions and having them come to Central Park caused quite a bit of disruption to our normal routines – repeating the exercise would get in the way of Super League commitments.

The biggest problem Wigan faced was winning possession, which was really all down to the forwards; we always knew that if we managed to get some ball we were capable of scoring tries. We thought that it was possible for us to win, but I believed that whether we did or not would depend on the type of game that Bath played. If they were prepared to play an open game we had a chance, but if they kept it tight, using their forwards to set up rucks and mauls, we would struggle.

By the time the whistle blew to start the game at Twickenham the pressure had really started to mount, and I think it got to us. To begin with we tried to play Rugby Union: we kicked for position and so gave possession away, instead of holding on to the ball. This was a mistake, because it was a type of game that was alien to most of the Wigan players – it proved very frustrating at the time, but we just had to come to terms with it. I felt that we could have done better, but some of the players were apprehensive about going into rucks and mauls, simply because they weren't sure what to do. And when we lost Scott Quinnell, our most experienced Rugby Union forward, early on in the game, we were really up against it.

Eventually we reverted to trying to play League – that meant keeping the ball in hand wherever possible and avoiding taking the ball into contact situations, which would result in the formation of rucks and mauls. When we were under pressure we tried to run our way out of trouble instead of just kicking the ball. It seemed to work, because we ended up scoring some spectacular tries, two of which began behind our own line. Considering that we also had a couple of tries disallowed, I don't think we did do too badly in losing 44–19. Playing under Union laws had been a challenge for us, but Bath did what they had to do – it showed just how different the two games are.

The match against Bath at Twickenham fired my enthusiasm and made me want to give Union a try again. I'd played against the best Rugby Union team in the country, so I definitely thought I could give the game a go. After all, I'd grown up with Rugby Union, and the fact that it was now professional presented me with interesting options. The advent of Super League meant that Rugby League in Britain was now a summer sport, so it wasn't possible to play in Australia during the off-season any more – something I'd managed on a couple of occasions – because the two seasons were running concurrently.

My contract with Wigan had three more years to run, but I didn't know what the future held for me after that. But Rugby Union was a much bigger game, nationally and internationally, and I thought going back to it would open up a lot of new possibilities. I love playing Rugby League and it has many attractions, but Union represented a new challenge. My idea was that if I could get back to Union, and possibly win a cap for England, my name would become known much more widely. It would really be something to play in the Five Nations and score a try – and I reckoned that if I managed to score half the tries in Union that I'd scored in League it would be a real achievement. If a winger runs the length of the field to score a try in Rugby Union it's considered special, but I've done that quite a few times in League, so the chance to do something like it was appealing. The trouble is that running the length of the field in Union is easier said than done, because the two extra players on each side meant that there's far more cover in the game.

There are quite a few other differences, too: as I said, they're different games. For example, there have been times in League when I've known that my performance has been the difference between winning and losing a game. But in Union it would be harder for me to say that. You can't simply go in, get the ball and score a try – the game's just not like that – whereas in Rugby League you are guaranteed a certain amount of possession and can seize the initiative.

Rugby League is much more highly structured than Union, as well, and it's become a lot more structured since I first played the game at Widnes. In those days we had lots of moves, but we tended to play off the cuff; now League has become more like a game of chess. In fact, if there were no errors then it would be the most simple, basic game ever invented. What happens is that on the fifth tackle a team kicks to the corner, the opposition full-back retrieves it and then takes a tackle. Next the winger takes another tackle, the forwards take it on for two more drives, and then there may be a back-line move: if nothing materialises, you kick down-field; their full-back retrieves it; and the same process starts all over again. You sometimes see this sequence in Test matches, for example, when all that's happening is that each side is waiting for the other one to make a mistake. In fact, the perfect game of Rugby League would be really boring. But it's not like that, because there are so many variables: if the ball goes into touch, for example, there'll be a different pattern of play from the resulting scrum. And, of course, nobody's perfect – mistakes do happen.

What moves you try as part of the sequence depends on where the ball is on the pitch. Generally, the nearer you are to your own try-line, the simpler the moves are, because it's vital that nobody drops the ball. The key elements in Rugby League are ball possession and defence, because unlike Rugby Union you can't deny the opposition the ball: you've only got six chances, and if you don't score you have to hand the ball over.

Tony Currie, the London Broncos' Coach, works things out mathematically. He says that to play well you have to complete around 75 per cent of your sets-of-six, and in an average game you will have about 20 sets-of-six per half. Each one takes about 40 seconds to complete, so any that you don't complete mean that the opposition has that much more time in possession – and that means you will have to do more defending and put in more tackles, which is the most tiring thing you do. No matter how great a side you are, you won't win the game if you don't complete a high percentage of your sets-of-six. When the London Broncos beat the Canberra Raiders, for example, the Raiders only completed nine out of their 19 sets-of-six in the first half, so even though they were a better side than us, we beat them.

Of course, Rugby Union is structured as well, and if you have a dominant pack it's possible to deny the opposition the ball: all you do is win the ball at the set pieces and kick it into touch. And even though your opponents may win a line-out they will be under such pressure that they have to kick – and you'll win the ball back at the next line-out. That's why England has been so dominant over the last few years: they've had such a good pack. And while League forwards take the ball on with a couple of drives before the backs try a move, so too do Union forwards: they drive on to set up rucks and mauls, using them as a springboard from which backs can attack when the defence is on the back foot or kick into touch.

The most important players in a Union team have always been the forwards, with the half-backs next in line. They're the ones who have all the options and have to make decisions about what to do in a certain situation: whether to kick; go to ground; stay on your feet; pass left or right; and so on. In Union the priority seems to be to establish a good field position, say in the opposition's 22, and then attack from there. The result is that you're talking about 10- to 15-yard breaks at the most. League is a much simpler game. It's a lot harder physically, it's true – you've got to be fast and strong –but far fewer decisions have to be made.

A lot of the games I played for Bedford weren't as intense as those I've played in Rugby League and I haven't been involved overall as much as I would have been in League. I still feel that when all's been said and done I'm a try scorer, and I would have been bored silly if I'd spent my whole career in Union. Take Rory Underwood, who holds the record for most tries scored for England: 49 in 85 appearances. I have only played 33 times for Great Britain, but I've scored 26 tries so my tries per game rate is far higher, simply because of the nature of the game.

One of the differences between League and Union that's struck me is that I really believe that your destiny is in your own hands in Rugby League, because you can play a good game even if you're in a bad side. So a player that performs well consistently can still achieve international honours: as I said, I was awarded my first Great Britain cap just five months after taking the game up. It wouldn't matter if you were Jonah Lomu, you still wouldn't get to the top that quickly in Union – it just doesn't happen like that. I think that's one of the down-sides of the sport, and it's one of the reasons I turned to Rugby League in the first place. Even today there seems to be more politics in Rugby Union: for example, how could England leave Jeremy Guscott out a few months before he was considered good enough for the Lions tour? Rugby League is a more down-to-earth honest game: if you're good enough you play and if you're not, you don't. And off the field, people don't seem to be too aware of many officials in Rugby League – apart from Maurice Lindsay – but in Rugby Union there seem to be hundreds of them.

Another difference is that Rugby Union, on the whole, is way behind Rugby League in terms of professionalism. League is a totally professional environment with a fully professional squad and Union just isn't. At many clubs, half the players are professional and half aren't; for me the switch in codes was like going from a completely professional environment to an amateur one. I've already spoken about the difference in training methods: one conducted by professionals and based on science; the other hit-and-miss, lacking in intensity and often supervised by schoolteachers. Things have improved. Off the field, the organisation has improved a lot since I was at Rosslyn Park, but it's still not as good as it was at Wigan – but then that's a hard act to follow.

But which game is the better, Union or League? People often ask me that, but I never like to get into the argument because both of them are good games. All I'll say is that in my heart I'm a Rugby League player, but I still enjoyed the challenge of playing Rugby Union.

11
Coming Home

Having made a successful career out of moving north and playing Rugby League, I'd always assumed that anything that I did in the future would stem from the game and that I'd stay in the North of England. But once the opportunity arose for me to come back to London I grabbed it with both hands. I liked life in the North – the people up there are easy to get on with and I'd made lots of friends –but increasingly I was looking at London as the place to be, and the perfect base from which to build a career outside of rugby.

But although I was born in Hackney, much of my early life was spent away from London. In fact, I've never been that fond of London: the only time I used to really like being there was from five at night to nine in the morning; once I moved up North my visits home would rarely last longer than 48 hours. It's a great place if you have money and want to enjoy yourself, but otherwise I just find it too intense: there's too much traffic and stress; and I'd hate to have a job in the city and have to go to work on the Tube every day. Nevertheless, I knew that there would be so many more opportunities for me in London. I'd be able to embark on a new challenge on the pitch, with the

London Broncos and Bedford, and advance my career outside rugby at the same time.

Even so, it felt a bit like coming home when I moved back to London: my family still lived there; and whenever Wigan had come down to London for cup finals we'd stay in a hotel in East London and be taken to Wembley by coach – we had to drive through Hackney, and I used to bore everyone on the bus by pointing out where I lived. But life back in London took a bit of getting used to: essentially, I had to rediscover the place. For the first few months, while I was playing for the Broncos and Bedford, I lived in a hotel in the centre of town. It was fun at first, but the novelty soon wore off, so I moved into a friend's flat in Cricklewood in October, and then moved into a place of my own in Chiswick, in January 1997. And gradually I settled in to London and got to know my way around. I've never been short of things to do, and being involved with companies like the CSI modelling agency means I'm always inundated with invitations to movie premieres, concerts and celebrity parties, where I get to meet some of my favourite pop stars.

CSI is owned by my girlfried Zara, Lennox Lewis and his business manager Panos Eliades. So along with my obvious connection with Frank Warren this means I get to see a lot of boxing; and because of the Bedford and London Broncos connections the likes of Steve Collins have even been spotted both at Goldington Road and The Stoop.

There was a lot of publicity when I signed for the Broncos and Bedford. The headlines in the papers were all related to the London Broncos – the Bedford deal, which was actually more important in terms of the number of games I would play, seemed to be played down – and for the second time in my career I made ITV's *News at Ten*. I don't know how much the Broncos paid for me as a transfer fee, but I should think they more than recouped their outlay because I reckon they've had about £300,000-worth of publicity since I signed. I was certainly here, there and everywhere on their behalf, so I think they got their money's worth.

I wasn't really surprised at the hype surrounding my signing for the Broncos because I knew that the fact that I was coming down to London was a big story, but the one thing that did take me back a little was the press conference and the subsequent photo shoot of me with the London Broncos jersey. The press conference was held in a hotel just off Oxford Street, but we had to go outside to a nearby park for the pictures, and as I was walking round a whole host of photographers and film crews was following me. That's not something I've experienced too often – once or twice in Australia, maybe, but never in this country.

I signed on 2 August, and there was time for just two training sessions before the next home game, against Warrington. For the first week before moving to a more central location in town, I was staying at a hotel in Croydon – it's in South London, miles away from the centre of town, and I hadn't had much reason to go to South London when I was young. I think the only time I'd ever been there was to go clubbing at a place called 'The Fridge', in Brixton, so I didn't know my way around, and, at the time, the Broncos were playing at Charlton Athletic's ground, which was also in South London, a long way away from my hotel.

The Broncos must have assumed that I knew my way around

London because I'd grown up here, so they left me to my own devices. But I ended up getting lost on the way to the ground and just drove round and round. It was getting later and later, and I'm sure that at some point they must have thought I'd done a runner and wasn't going to turn up. Eventually I got there, just in time for the kick-off. Everyone was getting changed and my kit was in a pile in the corner. There was a shirt there with my name on its back, a number 35, but putting it on was a bit strange as I had always worn a number 5. Somehow it didn't feel quite right.

I don't know why that should have been, because I didn't feel like that when I was transferred from Widnes to Wigan – but I suppose the difference was that when I went into the Wigan dressing room for the first time I already knew quite a few of the players. I really didn't know anyone at the Broncos: I was very much the new kid. And when I put that kit on it seemed like the point of no return. I hadn't really thought of myself as a Broncos player until I put on the jersey and ran out onto the pitch. But once I had done it, that was it.

I got through that first game all right, and then I played against Oldham and scored the winning try. But I could still feel the toe injury all the time, and I needed an injection to play in the next match, which was against Wigan. This was probably the hardest game for me, and the newspapers naturally wanted to know how I felt about playing against my old club. I made out that I was really looking forward to the game, but the truth is that I wasn't. For the first time in my career I didn't want to play a game, and it was one of the worst rugby experiences I've ever had. It was rather like being asked to play for the opposition in a school game because they're a man short, and having to play against your mates. But as a professional you have to play whether you like it or not – I also knew that if you don't play to the best of your abilities against a team like Wigan you can end up being embarrassed, and I didn't want that.

I was still struggling with my injury, but I almost scored early on in the game when Tony Rea put a diagonal kick over the Wigan line – unfortunately I landed over the dead-ball line after I'd gone up to catch it. We played really well in the first half and were level 6–6; and 15 minutes into the second half we were leading 9–6. But then Shaun Edwards, who hadn't made the starting line up, came off the bench to replace Craig Murdock and transformed the game. The first thing he did was to take a pass from Mick Cassidy and run 40 metres to score under the posts, and then the floodgates opened. We ended up losing 34–13, although I did manage to score a try near the end.

Normally I'm not a sentimental guy, but after the game I came close to tears because all the lads with whom I'd shared so many good times were there. I'm glad I didn't stand in the way of their championship ambitions. But the irony is that Wigan lost the Super League title to St Helens by just a point – and it was their drawn game with the London Broncos, a game I played in at Central Park before I'd signed for them, that proved decisive.

I don't know why but the only time I've ever really questioned my decision to leave Wigan was after that game. I kept wondering, 'Have I done the right thing?', though I surprised myself by thinking like that. The Broncos are a good bunch of lads, and it was just a question of seeing something that is great that you're no longer a part of. But I kept consoling myself by thinking that I had to look to the long term.

As I began to go out more in London, people began to recognise me and approach me, In fact, I was quite surprised at just how many people knew who I was – I'd been used to the idea that quite a few people knew my name, but that not many of them knew my face. Many of the ones who spoke to me only knew about Union and the England team, so they were intrigued when I explained that I was playing both Union and League. And I began to feel that my home was here after I'd moved my furniture down from Manchester: it seems to me that home is where your furniture is and the place where you keep all the things that are familiar to you. I feel a lot more comfortable when I've got my television and video with me.

I was kept busy in those early months with training, playing and travelling, and in some ways I think that I needed to be busy in order to settle in. I used to get home tired but happy, because everything was new and exciting and I felt that I was at the centre of things. Mick Hucknall, of Simply Red, had also moved from Manchester to Surrey – I'd met Mick in Manchester and become friendly with him – and I often go over to his house to watch the football or go out somewhere with him. I was quite surprised how knowledgeable he was about Rugby League and the things that I'd done in the game.

I also began to see more of Lennox Lewis. I first met him when Frank Maloney, his manager, invited me to the occasion at which he was crowned officially as WBC Champion, and I see more of him now that I'm in London. I'm often mistaken for other sportsmen – people often ask me if I'm Ellery Hanley, or Eddie Newton, who plays for Chelsea – but once it happened to Lennox when I was out with him. We were at a Snoop Doggy Dog concert at Wembley Arena, and although we had seats at the back we wanted to be nearer the stage, so we started walking towards the front. Suddenly a large female bouncer grabbed hold of Lennox and stopped him. When he tried to explain to her she said: 'I don't know who you think you are Saracen, but you can't go down there.' I just wanted to burst out laughing: here was the heavyweight champion of the world and this woman thought he was one of the Gladiators. It made me feel better to think that things like this happen to really famous people, and not just to me.

While I was getting used to living in London, I also had to get used to playing in a new team. It's difficult to settle into a new environment because you want to impress everyone, and I was probably guilty of trying too hard in those early games for the Broncos. And my injury became worse, to the point at which eventually I had to stop playing because the toe was so painful. I thought that I did all right for the Broncos – I'd managed to score three tries in the four games that I played – but it was frustrating, because I knew I was capable of doing so much more for them.

Things started to calm down a bit when I started at Bedford. The club had finished bottom of the Second Division the previous season and was in the process of building a team capable of promotion to the First, so there was a lot of hard work to be done; also, there wasn't quite so much media exposure as I'd had with the Broncos. I didn't know too much about Bedford before I joined them, although I spent a day there looking around after the press conference to announce that I'd signed for them. I hadn't even met Paul Turner, the player-coach, or Geoff Cooke, the Director of Rugby, before I signed. I knew who they were of course; I'd played with Paul for the Penguins in the Hong Kong Sevens, ten years earlier, and Geoff Cooke was the former England manager and I'd bumped into him at various functions over the years. It was more Frank Warren's involvement that led me to join the club in the first place. I'd met Frank through boxing, and he had bought a stake in the club through his company, Sports Network Europe. Frank's a down-to-earth East End boy – not your typical Rugby Union type so I could relate to him – and most of his ventures have been successful, so I was sure that he would make a success out of Bedford.

Of course it would have been easier if I'd gone to a successful club that had a reputation for open, running rugby, like Bath or Harlequins. It's a lot harder to join a team that's rebuilding, but I thought that when things came right – as I'm sure they will for Bedford – it would be a lot more rewarding. And I thought that if I could bring some of the dynamism of League to Union, people might sit up and take notice. But it was much tougher to make an impact than I had thought.

When I first went to Bedford I felt like a professional in a very amateur environment and I soon realised that if I wanted to do anything I was going to have to do it for myself. At Wigan everything was done for you, whereas now I had to sort myself out. But I was prepared for that. Because Rugby Union had only recently become a fully professional sport the club was very much going into uncharted territory, and I knew that there would be teething problems.

I felt there was a lot of pressure on me when I joined, too – certainly from the spectators, because of my reputation – but I didn't know what I could do. It didn't help that I missed the start of the season because of my toe injury, and not being able to play or train was very frustrating, particularly when stories started to appear in the press questioning the decision to sign me. I was annoyed, because the only way I was going to prove them wrong was out on the pitch. Bedford had spent a lot of money on me, and all I seemed to be doing was getting them a lot of publicity, which I suppose was something given that the Division was being dominated by Richmond and Newcastle. I kept thinking, 'Surely they must have signed me for more than just the publicity.' There were snide remarks in the local press, and I wasn't happy just being there and not doing the things that I'd been doing in League. But things began to improve, and my job was to help the team to improve. I don't like being in a team that's playing badly and I don't like being in a side that's doing well if I'm not contributing.

One problem was that the atmosphere at Bedford was completely different to that at the Rugby League clubs I'd been with. There was a much more social feel to the place, and although Paul Turner worked very hard to bring in a more professional approach it was clear that things weren't going to change overnight. The majority of the players had played for fun before the game went professional, so it became a question of changing their attitude. And now that the club was paying players, it expected more from them: it wanted more of their time, and, of course, it expected results on the field.

Bedford expected more from me, too. They didn't see me as just another player; I was told, 'Martin, you have to be this guiding-light professional. Everyone's looking to you because you've been professional for ten years and they've only been professional for ten minutes.' But I wasn't the captain of the club, and nor did I have any special position. I was just a professional player like all the others yet they were asking different things of me. I had a bit of a problem with that at first, but Bedford paid my wages so I had to do what was right for them.

When I found that the club didn't have a sprint coach or a conditioning coach, as I'd expected there'd be, I decided to muck in and try to help. I took the sprint sessions for a time, but I didn't want to make too many suggestions because it can seem as though you think you know better than the people in charge. In fact, I didn't see eye to eye with Paul Turner and Geoff Cooke about a lot of things. At first I'd bite my lip and not say anything; but when I did say something it wasn't received in the right way.

One thing I found is that there are still players in Union whose skill levels aren't high enough and don't have sufficient commitment – and if everyone isn't giving 100 per cent, it's detrimental to the whole squad. Paul Turner is really committed to the club and to getting things done, but there are some players who probably aren't used to being at the top. For example, we lost our first game against Richmond by one point and I felt bad – but I noticed that, while some players weren't happy with the performance, they seemed reasonably pleased that we'd only just been beaten. I thought: 'We lost the game.' I hate seeing that bad team mentality in which you start to feel happy that you only lost by a point. That's not me: I had to pull myself up and stop thinking like that.

A Question of Style

A model professional.

Below left: *The Unusual Suspects. Wigan's chosen few, (left to right) Garry Connolly, me, Wes Cotton, Sean Long and Henry Paul, try to look cool on an Armani fashion shoot.*

Below: *Kilted-up and ready for action, an image which rugby league followers found hard to understand.*

Outside the Game

Above: *Speed kings. The line-up for the Martin Offiah Sprint Challenge which took place at Central Park in 1993 as part of Shaun Edwards's testimonial. The line-up is (left to right) Guy Bullock, the British 400 metre runner; local athlete Martin Hallsworth; Ade Mafe, the former European indoor 200 metre champion; Leicester rugby union wing Steve Hackney; rugby league players Eddie Rombo and Anthony Sullivan; me and Casualty star Patrick Robinson. We ran the length of the field and I won.*

Above: *Myself and Lennox Lewis having a top night out at my favourite club, Miss Moneypenny's in Birmingham, with co-owner Mick Ryan. As usual, Mick's brother Dermot was nowhere to be seen!*

Right: *Shaking hands with Mr Chariots of Fire himself, Colin Welland, who wrote the screenplay for the film.*

Above: *Down on the farm with my Emmerdale co-stars Big Mandy (Lisa Riley, on the left) and Tina (Jacqueline Pirie).*

Below: *Me with one of my best friends, Lee Garrick, one of the co-promoters at Miss Moneypenny's.*

Above: *On the set of* Hollyoaks *with Yasmin Bannerman, who plays Maddie Parker.*

Above: *Trying to take Dave Myers, a team-mate at both Widnes and Wigan, under my wing.*

Below: *Backstage with the girls, I get to meet one of my favourite groups, Eternal. Sometimes life is really tough for a rugby player!*

Rugby Reunion

Right: *The highlight of a tough first year back in union, scoring the winning try for Bedford against Newcastle at Goldington Road.*

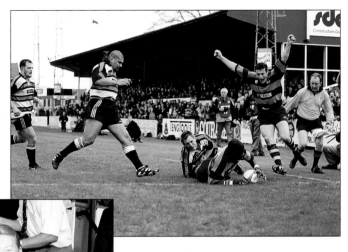

Left: *Sitting in the stand on the opening day of the rugby union season with boxing promoter and Bedford chairman Frank Warren, the man responsible for me joining the club.*

Right: *A rare sight in union, ball in hand in open space.*

The sign that said it all outside Goldington Road prior to my debut for Bedford.

Super League

Riding high as part of the Broncos' publicity machine.

Getting collared by Mateaki Mafi on my debut for the London Broncos against Warrington in August 1996.

Left: *Teaming up with Richard Branson to celebrate Virgin's sponsorship of the London Broncos.*

Right: *Welcoming my old friend Shaun Edwards to London with Broncos skipper Terry Matterson. It's great having Shaun in the side.*

Cross-Codes

Right: *Still flying as I show Harlequins wing Daren O'Leary a clean pair of heels in the 1996 Middlesex Sevens.*

Above: *Middlesex Sevens champions 1996, Wigan Rugby League.*

Right: *High-impact collision with rugby union's top hit-man, the Bath No.8 Steve Ojomoh, at Twickenham in the cross-code challenge in 1996.*

So, trying to be the 'guiding-light professional' I'd try to shake up the players who weren't used to the big time and were happy with second best. Sometimes they thought I was winding them up, but I think everyone should be a bit cocky – you need a certain degree of arrogance to be successful. If someone beats me during a game, for example, I'll make damn sure they don't do it again. I can understand that it's difficult for people to develop this attitude when they have been playing the game for the love of it all their lives, but things have to change in the professional era. We were at Bedford because we were good rugby players and had been chosen by the club to do a job, not because we happened to be a good bunch of blokes who wanted to play together – and the sooner everyone realised that the better. There's still what I call a 'turn up' mentality, but playing professional rugby isn't just about turning up and playing the game; it's about trying to better yourself and making the team better. Mind you, I find it hard myself to get motivated for friendly games, in which nothing is at stake except personal pride, with no league points and no cup glory. I'm used to playing for things that mean something.

The dressing room was different, too. Sometimes it felt like a League dressing room, particularly when Frank Warren came in before we played Newcastle and said: 'OK boys, the team is on a £20,000 bonus if you win.' That type of thing often happened in League before a big game; I asked, 'Is that each?' He chuckled and said, 'Martin, I might have expected that from you.' But generally there isn't the same openness of emotions in Union as you find in League: if two people in a League team didn't like each other, everyone would soon know about it. But in Union, things wouldn't be so obvious – I don't know whether that's to do with class and upbringing. Then again, there's a different etiquette in Rugby Union. I sometimes have a problem keeping quiet, and if something is really bugging me I'm the type of person who tries to get it out rather than suffer in silence. But in Union that's not always the best way to go about things – and that's not necessarily right or wrong, but just different. Issues tend to be dealt with by means of a quiet chat, whereas in League the players have a big meeting if they're not happy about something, to get it out in the open and deal with it.

I think that this habit of mine, carried over from League, led to me being thought of as a bit of a troublemaker at first, so I had to learn to bite my tongue at times. I don't want to sound too big headed, but I've been earning a six-figure salary since the day I joined Wigan, in 1992, so it's difficult to sit there sometimes when someone's talking to you as if you're a child, asking you to feel grateful for being paid. But I'm not one to say, 'This is what you should do,' even though it may be tempting. Paul Turner has said things to me and I've thought, 'You'd better be quiet Martin, this is Rugby Union not Rugby League.' I didn't want to be seen as someone who comes in and thinks he knows it all, but I am pretty opinionated and I remember Paul Turner saying once: 'Martin, you've got an answer for everything.' But if I truly believe something is wrong, I find it hard not to say so. In Rugby League you would just say 'What are you doing that for?', but in Union there's still this idea that you have to keep your mouth shut because you're getting paid for something that you used to do for nothing. I've had to adjust: now I can see other people's points of view, and I try to do the best I can, even if I don't agree with them.

A typical example of what I mean occurred soon after I arrived at the London Broncos: the players said that the gym they were using was too far away, and complained about the fact. The club listened, and resolved the problem, because it wanted to help. But the attitude in Rugby Union is very different: the belief is that you can tell the players to do anything, because you're paying them: so if the club says that you have to be up at three o'clock in the morning and travel 1,200 miles to train, so be it. That's not the way it should be: a club should do as much as possible to help the players rather than making life hard for them. Things are beginning to change, but a lot of egos were bruised during the transition from the old amateur days to the new professional era. I suppose it's because members have done things for the club over the years not because they've been paid or because they're the best people for the job, but because they wanted to be associated with Bedford – and that goes for the players, too. But in Rugby League, everyone, from the players to the groundsman, is there because it's their job. That's the essential difference between an amateur set-up and a professional one.

Bedford are certainly pushing towards a professional set-up, and I could see a lot of things that I think would work there – but I wasn't the coach. I found many things frustrating, but if I made any criticisms people could just turn round to me and say, 'You may be a Rugby League international, but this is Rugby Union.' That was never actually said, but sometimes if a player like Steve McCurrie, who used to be at Widnes, dropped a ball or made a mistake in training you would hear people say, 'We expect more from Rugby League players.'

Eventually I put all this behind me when I made my first-team debut at home against Rotherham, on 19 October. It's hard to put what I felt when I played that first game for Bedford into words. I was trying to remember what Union had been like last time I played it, but it was so long since I'd played in a Union team that I found it impossible. I just tried to approach the game in the same way that I used to approach League games. All I wanted to do was to get my hands on the ball and score a try – and, thankfully, that's just what I did.

But things were difficult in those first few games, because the team didn't know how to use me and I didn't know the best way of involving myself in the play so that I could make a positive impact. At first, playing Union again was pretty difficult, because I had to learn to read the game all over again. Following the ball is something of a sixth sense with me, but Paul Turner told me that there were certain habits that I would have to try and unlearn, and that was one of them – I thought that was a bit of a challenge. I tried to apply some of the methods I'd learned in League to Union, and some of them worked while others failed. I used to say, 'If I did that in League, it would have been a certain score,' but I knew that I was playing a different game.

I didn't start off too badly, though: I scored tries in the first few games and two against Moseley. But after that I didn't seem to do anything. That's when people started saying, 'We've spent all this money on him and what has he done?' I'm not the type of player whose performance can be measured by how many tackles I make in a game. Spectators tend to be very fickle, though: I could have the same type of game two weeks running, and go from being someone who shouldn't even be on the pitch to being one of the greatest players they've ever seen – and the difference may well have been that a gap was an inch wider, or someone missed my ankles by a whisker. My view is that I must be one or the other, but I can't be both: you don't go from being brilliant to terrible in the space of a week.

Sometimes I wondered whether I'd done the right thing by going from a sport in which I was scoring lots of tries to one in which the wing position probably isn't as important. In League, a good winger can really turn the game on its head by scoring tries, but in Union it's normally the team with the bigger, more dominant pack that has the largest influence on the game. The opportunities for wingers tend to be few and far between, and you have to be a lot more patient. But, perhaps because of all the publicity when I'd signed for Bedford, I thought I had to score amazing tries all the time – that was what I'd been used to doing. I'd never gone more than three games without scoring a try in League, but I went four games without scoring at Bedford. I had to keep reminding myself I was playing a different game.

For me to be happy and playing well I've got to be confident: wingers are very insecure people, and if I'm not scoring tries my confidence suffers. Even some of the players pointed out that I didn't seem to be enjoying myself – and I wasn't, because the tries weren't coming. The way we trained didn't help: everyone who's played with me knows that I take the mickey at training by trying to take people on and going round them on the outside to try to gee them up bit. If we were playing touch rugby at Wigan and one player made a bit of a fool of another, the other player would be determined that it wouldn't happen again. But there doesn't seem to be the same attitude in

Union, and I think that they took what I was doing the wrong way. But for me to play well I've got to be myself, and I need to be confident and cocky. My attitude was: 'If you don't like me, get rid of me'.

So the early period at Bedford was frustrating. Even though I hadn't played Rugby Union for a long time, and I realise I'm not the most complete player in the world, I do know there are certain things I can do and do them well – and if I'm not doing them then there's no point in me being there. I'm sure that I'd have been scoring tries if I had been on the end of a Bath or Harlequins back-line that was creating chances. I may not know much, but I am confident in my own ability to score tries; I've done that against the best, in both codes and at all levels.

Sometimes it's hard to be open and honest. I began to think: 'Should I be myself or do what the coaches want?' But, on the other hand, people want you to be a player who makes decisions: you can't be subservient and not say anything. It brought home to me just how very different Rugby Union is to Rugby League.

I had a few run-ins with Geoff Cooke and Paul Turner, one of which resulted in me receiving a written warning. Although Union had gone professional, even the full-time players only trained at the club on Tuesdays and Thursdays – yet they were expected to train during the day and then attend the sessions with the full squad in the evening. When I first started, there was just a handful of us: me; Junior Paramore; Mick Pechey; Ben Whetstone; Mike Rayer; and Steve McCurrie. In the morning we'd do a weights session in the gym and then some ball work, before finishing around one o'clock; if someone was injured, or had something else to do – which happened quite often – there'd only be three of us, and it was impossible to do any meaningful work. So we'd have at least six hours off before coming back at seven to do a full squad session with people like Jeff Probyn and Norm Hadley, who still had jobs.

A lot of the players lived in Bedford and it was easier for them, but I lived an hour-and-a-half's drive away, which could turn into three when the traffic was bad, and it wasn't really worth going home and coming back – so I just had to hang around. I used to go to Pizza Hut and have a long lunch, or go to the cinema – I saw so many films during my season at Bedford that I could have got a job as a movie critic. Paul Turner was great, and used to invite me round to his house, but you can't really relax anywhere but your own home and it's essential, as every professional sportsman knows, that you rest properly in the afternoon if you've trained in the morning. The upshot was that every Tuesday and Thursday I'd do three training sessions and I'd get back home about 10 pm and then be up at 8.30 the next morning to go training.

When I said that I wasn't too happy about this situation, in the presence of Paul Turner and a lot of the other players, I was reminded about my contract, which stated that I should be living in Bedford anyway. But the original contract, which did stipulate that, was drawn up when I was just looking for a short-term deal. However, when Wigan said they were prepared to release me permanently, and I signed to play for Bedford and the London Broncos, I'd told Frank Warren that I couldn't live in the town because it would be too far from the Broncos' base at Crystal Palace: I needed to live somewhere within striking distance of both Bedford and the Broncos.

I thought that Geoff Cooke could have just had a word with me about the whole business, but instead I got a written warning: it said that I had to turn up for all training sessions.

I was looking forward to playing Rugby League again for the Broncos at the start of the 1997 Super League season, and after a couple of training sessions I soon got back into the groove: it was like putting on a pair of old, comfortable slippers. The Broncos had moved to the Harlequins ground, in Twickenham, which was handy for me, and I soon got to know all the lads, the majority of whom are Australian. I've played in Sydney and been to Australia about eight times, so I know all about the Aussies – I like their sense of humour, and I really enjoy it down there. I had a good, hard week of training before I played my first game of the season for them, against St Helens, though I was quite nervous about it because I hadn't played League for about seven months – the longest I'd ever been away from the game. But I really enjoyed it, and though we lost, by 28–24, I scored a try.

In fact, I was enjoying myself all round, as we proved that the previous season's fourth place in the Super League wasn't a flash in the pan, and I ended up playing three games for the Broncos in the early part of the season instead of the two for which I was contracted. And when Bedford didn't have a game over the Easter weekend, and the Broncos were playing Paris St Germain at the Stoop on Good Friday, I scored a hat-trick in the 28–10 win. I was glad that I did, because I wanted to make amends for my disappointing game against Warrington, on the weekend when I played both League and Union.

The club's got a decent squad of players and an excellent

coach: Tony Currie is the first one I've played under who has a nickname – 'TC'. In fact, I've played against him a couple of times, and he was in the Australian team when Great Britain won that historic Third Test in Sydney, in 1988. I think it's very hard for coaches to be liked and respected, but he certainly is. I've got a lot of time for Tony: he seems to get his point across without too many words, but if something isn't right he'll come and tell you – he's very similar in that way to John Monie.

I tried to get Shaun Edwards to come down to the Broncos soon after I signed for them. His contract with Wigan was coming up for renewal and at the time he wanted to stay, but he wasn't getting into the team because Craig Murdock was playing at scrum-half. Shaun was forced to sit on the bench for weeks, and there was talk that the club didn't need him any more. He was nearing 30 and he was being paid a lot of money. I realised what a valuable player he was, and said that if Wigan didn't want him then the Broncos certainly did. And when the Broncos played Wigan in London that season, he was on the bench and Wigan were struggling – but when he came on he completely changed the game and was responsible for winning the match for them. I said as much in interviews afterwards, and I think that Wigan realised how valuable he was to them after that game because he was offered another contract.

But the situation changed the following year, because Heather, his girlfriend, was having a baby and he wanted to be with her in London; he wasn't getting on with Graeme West, either, and the team was struggling. I told him that the Broncos would be interested in him joining them, but Wigan said that they wanted a transfer fee for him. But if anyone deserved a free transfer it was Shaun: he'd signed for Wigan on his 17th birthday, and been a great servant to the club. Thankfully, the problems were resolved, and it's been great having him at the Broncos, because he's just the kind of player that the club needs.

It took a while for the team to get used to Shaun, though, because he can be a bit weird: sometimes in training, for example, he just jogs round the pitch on his own. And four weeks after coming down to London he said to me: 'It's the worst decision I've made in my life. I want to go back up North.' I think that was just after Wigan had battered us 38–10 at Central Park; they had their full squad back and were doing well. But a couple of months later we beat them at The Stoop, then we hammered the Canberra Raiders in the World Club Championship – and Shaun was all smiles again. He had landed on his feet.

I think having Shaun and I helps the Broncos, because we are two players who are used to winning: we've come from an environment in which it was normal to win big games, and I think that tends to rub off on other players. It's easier for Shaun to do what he does when I'm around, and there's no doubt that he's had a tremendous influence on the Broncos. It can't be just coincidence that he keeps coming on to the pitch and turning games round. His secret is to get people doing the things that they should be doing. For example, some players start to panic if they're in the lead with 15 minutes to go and start playing for time, but Shaun will just say, 'Don't worry about the end of the game, don't even think about it. Just keep doing what you're doing and work hard.' And then the final whistle has gone before you know it.

After playing those three games for the Broncos it was back to Bedford until the end of their season. Richmond were at the head of the table, and we were pushing for promotion, together with Newcastle. But then it was announced that there would be a play-off between the sides that finished third and fourth from the bottom of the First Division, and the teams that finished third and fourth from the top of the Second Division: the winners would play in the First Division the following season; and the losers would play in the Second. Although we were lying second in the table, I felt that we were in a false position. We'd played a lot more games than Newcastle, who were just below us. But when we played them at Bedford, on 5 April, we turned in one of our best performances of the season, and beat them 34–28.

After that result everyone assumed that we were going to go through the rest of the season without losing a game, but it didn't work out like that. Suddenly we were the big guns up there to be shot at, but even after the win over Newcastle I still didn't think we were good enough for the top flight – if we played them ten times I think that they would have beaten us eight times. Frank Warren bet £50,000 on us winning promotion, but he was more confident than I was. We lost our next league game 40–34, at Moseley; and then we lost at home to London Scottish, by 28–14. And Coventry beat us by 30–10 in our final league fixture – hardly the form you'd expect from a side with aspirations to First Division status.

It's difficult to pinpoint what went wrong, but sometimes it's hard to reach the level of intensity again after you've peaked for a big game: it's difficult to reach the same emotional high. Raising yourself again demands so much effort that it's sometimes physically impossible to achieve it, and we simply weren't able to stoke the fires again. Everyone kept saying: 'Forget about the Newcastle game,' but the very fact that it was mentioned so many times made it impossible for us to get it out of our minds. In hindsight it may have been better for us to have played well against Newcastle and lost the game.

We ended up fourth in the Second Division, behind Richmond, Newcastle and Coventry, which meant that we had to take on Bristol, who had ended up fourth from bottom of the First Division, in the play-offs. We were to play them both home and away, and the outcome was to be decided by the aggregate score of the two matches. We knew that we had to really motivate ourselves for the two games if we were to stand any chance of promotion.

The first game was at Goldington Road, and although we didn't play particularly well and we picked up a few injuries we only lost 20–11 – so we still had a chance. But we went down 19–12 in the return match at Bristol: they were simply too good for us, and had so many quality players, such as the England and Lions lock Simon Shaw and Robert Jones, the former Wales scrum-half. So that wrapped up my season back in Rugby Union – it meant that Bedford would be playing Second Division rugby again next season.

I ended up as Bedford's second highest try-scorer with 13, behind Ben Whetstone, who had 21. I didn't think that was bad, considering that I missed so many games through injury at the beginning of the season and I didn't play a full game in quite a few of the others. It was tough to begin with, but you just have to look at it as a job and be professional about it. Of all the games I played, the ones I enjoyed the most were those against the big teams, like Bristol and Newcastle. I found it easier to motivate myself for those matches, because there was usually a big crowd and a good atmosphere, whereas at some of the clubs we played that was distinctly lacking.

On reflection, my season at Bedford was a lot more disappointing than I had anticipated, but I think the problem was that my expectations had been too high. I had to re-think my priorities during the season, and I decided not to place as much emphasis on try scoring and concentrate on my other jobs instead – but if I got a scoring opportunity I'd take it. Before this, I was pulling my hair out if I didn't get the ball and have any opportunities to score: it was getting me down. But I think that playing Rugby League again for a couple of weeks gave me a boost of confidence, because I scored a try in each of Bedford's next six games when I came back to Union.

But if I'm honest, I have to say that there were times after I'd signed for Bedford when I sat down and thought, 'What have I done?' I still had a three-year contract at Wigan and I could have stayed there, but I think that going to Bedford and Union was the best thing I could have done. They were the only ones who offered me a good contract, and I'm at the stage of my career at which I don't really have to go to somewhere like Harlequins and prove myself, because I know exactly what I'm able to do.

It was good to see at first hand how Union is becoming a lot more dynamic and a lot faster. I came off the pitch after some games and thought: 'That was really enjoyable' – and that's far more important. No matter how much money you're getting paid to do something, you just don't want to do it if it's mundane and boring. And I think that Union will become even faster and more dynamic: there appears to be less kicking now than there was when I first played the game, especially at club level. It'll probably never be as dynamic as League, because of the nature of the game, but it has certainly become a lot more intense.

I've watched games involving sides such as Bath and Leicester, whereas I wouldn't have bothered watching club games before, and I think that the game is definitely improving as a spectacle. It's changing a lot, particularly with so many big international stars, like François Pienaar, Joel Stransky and Philippe Sella, coming into the British game. The only problem is the relative lack of atmosphere at the grounds. I still see League as the big summer spectacular that is great to watch, but Union is still seen as the number one code of rugby. I can't see the two codes coming together, unless someone like Rupert Murdoch wants it to happen. I think there's too much resistance from the powers-that-be in each sport, so the games will remain separate.

Overall, I enjoyed my time with Bedford. I had some problems in the early days, but by the end of the season I was getting on with Paul Turner very well – he's a great admirer of Rugby League, and one of the most knowledgeable men about rugby that I've ever met.

It's also been a pleasure to work with a full-back as talented as Mike Rayer. I remember watching him a couple of times when he played for Cardiff and Wales, and thinking that he was big, fat and slow, but nothing could be further from the truth. He's a lot quicker than most people think and has an amazing side-step and dummy – second only to Jonathan Davies – that seems to work all the time. When we called moves involving Mike, gaps used to just open up for him and he'd score a try under the posts. He's an amazingly good player, and in my opinion he was one of the best full-backs in the country last season.

There are positives and negatives in everything, and I try to look for the positives. They are that I've learned a lot, and I'm a better player now after having a season playing Union in the Second Division. And I'm really enjoying living in London, and I don't have any regrets about moving.

12
My Mad
Weekend

A number of Rugby League players took advantage of the breaking down of the barriers between League and Union to take up short-term contracts with Rugby Union clubs at the end of the first Super League season, in September 1996. But I had a different type of arrangement: my deal committed me first and foremost to Bedford, and my contract with the London Broncos was secondary – although under the terms of the agreement I had to play 12 Super League games for the Broncos, including the first two of the season.

Both clubs were aware of the situation and agreed these terms before the deals went through. Of course Bedford and the London Broncos have independent fixture lists, so they could hardly arrange their seasons so that my absences would not be felt. And with the 1997 Super League season due to start on 14 March a clash was inevitable. I knew that I would have to break off from Bedford's Second Division promotion race to join up with the Broncos for the first two games, but I didn't anticipate having to play a League match and a Union match on consecutive days!

The first Broncos game was against St Helens on 16 March

at the Stoop. It was to be televised live by Sky Sports on the Sunday evening, and, fortunately for me, there was no Bedford fixture that weekend – so everything worked out perfectly. But on the second weekend of Super League the Broncos were scheduled to play a game at Warrington on Friday evening, once again in front of the Sky Sports cameras. I don't think it was a coincidence that the first two Broncos games were televised; after all, I still had a contract with Super League and needed its approval to play Rugby Union for Bedford, and it was Super League that had stipulated that I had to play the first two league games for the Broncos.

But as luck would have it, Bedford were due to play a Second Division game at Rotherham the day after the Super League game at Warrington. We were lying second in Division Two and pushing hard for promotion, and Rotherham were in the top half of the table – so they weren't going to be pushovers, particularly on their own ground. Now it was very clear from my contract that I was a London Broncos player for that weekend, and I would have been quite within my rights to say that there was no way I could play for Bedford, but I decided to look at the situation positively.

Paul Turner asked me: 'What do you think about playing two games this weekend, Martin?' My reply was, 'I'm up for it. If it can be done I'll do it. It will be something unique.' But what I didn't realise at the time was that I was to receive my MBE from Prince Charles at Buckingham Palace on the Friday of the Warrington game. When I found out about that, I wondered just how I was going to get to Warrington in time to play for the Broncos, so I rang my agent Alan McColm to say, 'What am I going to do now?'

I had been awarded the MBE in the New Year's Honours List at the beginning of the year. Quite a few Rugby League players had received gongs over the years, such as Ellery Hanley, Shaun Edwards, Garry Schofield and Jonathan Davies, and I must admit that when I started doing well and breaking records I thought that I might possibly be in line for the honour. And around the time I moved from Wigan to London the Prime Minister's office sent me a letter telling me that my name had been put forward to the Her Majesty The Queen recommending me for an MBE, and asking if I would accept the award if it was granted. The trouble was that it was sent to my old house in Manchester, and I didn't receive it until November. Of course I replied that I would accept the award if it was offered – but I decided not to tell anyone about it, because I thought that if I did something would go wrong. So I kept the news from my friends and family. It was really difficult – I don't know how I managed it.

I had been training at Bedford on New Year's Eve, and when I turned on my mobile phone on my way back to London I found that all the message space had been taken up. All the calls were from journalists who wanted to speak to me urgently, so I realised that it could only be about one thing – it gave me a bit of a tingle. But I still didn't know for sure, so I contacted Martin Richards, of the *Daily Mirror*, and he told me that I'd been awarded the MBE. I got constant requests for interviews after that, and the honour seemed to mean a lot to everyone I spoke to about it. It meant a lot to me, too – when I was younger it seemed that only elevated people in the establishment received honours like this. What's more, it was good to get recognition outside my sport and to have those letters after my name. I suppose it meant that my career had amounted to something.

But I was now faced with the problem: how could I collect my award on Friday 21 March, play Rugby League at Warrington that same evening and play Rugby Union at Rotherham the next day? Nobody had ever played both codes at that level on consecutive days, so it would certainly be unique – but the trip to the Palace certainly complicated things. I like challenges, though, and the idea certainly captured the attention of the media: television crews and reporters were planning to follow my every move over the weekend. But the main problem lay in the logistics of the exercise. It was too risky to drive from place to place, or to use public transport, so how could I get from one place to another? I left the problem with Alan, and he contacted the Broncos.

One thing about the London Broncos, especially now that Richard Branson is on board, is that they're very good at public relations – I've done more PR work in a year for the London Broncos than I have done for any other club. And the Broncos saw my mad weekend as a golden opportunity for some publicity. So I just left all the arrangements up to Alan and the Broncos. Their Richard Branson connection led the Broncos to come up with the idea of using a Virgin helicopter to take me from London to Manchester Airport, and from there I would be able to get to Warrington in time for the game. The plan was to stay in Manchester overnight after the match, and then drive over to Rotherham on Saturday morning to meet up with the Bedford team and play for them that afternoon.

That still left quite a lot for me to do, because obviously the London Broncos and Bedford weren't in communication.

I had to hire a car and find somewhere to stay while I was up North, and although Alan helped out it was basically all down to me. The only down side of all this was that the whole thing was becoming a bit of a circus, and whenever that happens things tend to backfire on me. I do find it hard to keep mentally focused when I have too much attention from the media before a game. By now I was more worried about getting my MBE at the Palace and going up in the helicopter than about playing in the games of rugby.

I had arranged for a limousine to pick me up, together with my mother and Zara, my girlfriend, from my home in Chiswick on the Friday morning. I was ready early, dressed in my morning suit, complete with top hat and gloves, and the car arrived around nine o'clock and we got to the Palace at about ten. I had been there a few months before for a get-together of sports people and had met most of the Royal Family – although not Prince Charles, who was due to present me with my MBE. Once our car had been searched, we met up with a representative of the Nigerian High Commission. Many of the black rugby players, such as Victor Ubogu and Steve Ojomoh, are Nigerian because so many Nigerian children are sent to school over here and learn the game, and there had been a certain amount of publicity in Nigeria about my career.

I was ushered into a big room that had paintings of Kings and Queens round the walls and was full of people who were to be presented with a variety of awards: MBEs, OBEs, CBEs, and knighthoods. They were all in separate groups, rather like sheep in a pen, and I remember chatting with Steve Redgrave, whom I'd met before. That put me a little more at ease, but the whole business seemed to take ages. While we were waiting we were taken through the protocol – how to receive the award and how to address Prince Charles – and told not to speak unless spoken to. They explained that at a certain point the Prince would put his hand out and that would be our signal to leave, so I would shake his hand, bow and then back off – because you're not allowed to turn your back on him. All that sounds very formidable, but in fact the whole business was very simple and painless. Prince Charles told me that he'd played second-row at school, and said that I was very sensible to have stayed out on the wing and avoided the pack.

Afterwards I met up with my mother and my girlfriend and posed for photographs. A few television crews were there, and the reporter from Sky TV said: 'Can we have your mum?' At first she thought that they just wanted her to stand next to me, looking all happy and radiant, but then they put a microphone in front of her. She usually shies away from anything like that, but they must have caught her off guard – she did very well and said how happy she was. Then it was back home to get changed and grab something to eat before being driven off to Battersea Heliport. As you know, I don't like flying, and I'd never been in a helicopter before, so I tried not to think about the flight until I was actually at the heliport. I though that the journey would take about half-an-hour, but they told me that it would take an hour and a half to get to Manchester. I couldn't believe it.

We took off around four o'clock and flew low along the Thames, which didn't make me happy at all. But things got better as we headed out into the countryside, and, while I wouldn't go as far as to say it was enjoyable, it became quite pleasant. I started talking to the pilot, and the more I talked the more I relaxed – although I remember a plane flying past at one point without any reaction from the pilot, and I wondered: 'Did he see that?' I was glad that I wasn't going back in the helicopter that evening: if I'd had the choice between being paid £1,000 to go back on it or playing against Rotherham for free, I'd opt to play against Rotherham any day.

By the time I got off the helicopter at Manchester Airport it was around 5.30 pm, and I was very relieved that I'd got there. I felt as if my day was over, but I still had a game to play so I tried hard to re-motivate myself on the drive to Warrington, but it wasn't easy. I arrived at the ground just after six o'clock, in good time for a seven-thirty kick-off, but I had to do some interviews before I could change and start preparing for the match with the rest of the lads. I suppose it's hardly surprising that the game that followed wasn't my best ever: the ball didn't really come my way, and by the time I got into the game there was only about ten minutes left. I was running around all over the pitch trying to get involved, because I felt I hadn't really done anything for the whole game. In fact, I think I only touched the ball about half-a-dozen times. But we managed to win, by 38–18.

I didn't feel too bad after the game, considering the day I'd had, but by the time I'd attended the press conference and been picked up by my mate Gareth, who was driving me to Manchester, it was after ten o'clock, and I was pretty tired. I'm glad I arranged for him to pick me up, because I wouldn't have liked to have driven myself. I must have arrived at the Midland Hotel at around 11 o'clock. We'd bumped into Andy Craig at

Warrington – he used to play at Wigan and had recently been transferred to Swinton – and he suggested that we go out for the night, but I said: 'I don't know where you've been, but I've got to play another game tomorrow.' He must have been the only person in the country who didn't know what I was doing that weekend. And there was no way I was going to take him back to his home in St Helens, so I said that he could use one of the twin beds in the room and stay the night. But we'd only been in bed for about half-an-hour when he decided he was going out after all and then came back late – so I didn't have the most restful of nights.

Gareth picked me up at the hotel in Manchester at nine-thirty in the morning and I discovered that the stereo wasn't working in the hire car. I didn't want to drive around all day without any music, so we took the car back and picked up another one, and then we set off for Rotherham – I could have done without the hassle. I'd bought a few papers to read on the way, and I was a bit surprised to read a report in the *Express* about what I was doing. The piece claimed that Geoff Cooke wasn't happy because he hadn't seen me for two weeks, and he was quoted as saying that he didn't think it was in the best interests of myself or Bedford to play in the game against Rotherham.

It's not very nice to read things like that in the newspapers, so I gave Alan a call. I assumed there had been a breakdown in communications, because Alan confirmed that it was in my contract, which everyone had signed back in August, that I would be playing for the Broncos that weekend. And Geoff Cooke must have seen the contract, because he quoted from it chapter and verse when he sent me that warning letter earlier in the season. I don't see why someone from Bedford couldn't just have rung me and said: 'Look Martin, you're with the London Broncos this weekend, so don't play for us,' but they didn't. I just decided to put it all to one side, however, and get on with things.

By the time I got to the team's hotel I was pretty tired and I just lounged around, trying to relax. Paul Turner told me I was on the bench – which I knew anyway, because Alan had told me – and I didn't have any problem with that. Unfortunately the guy playing on the wing, Marcus Cook, got injured, so I went on to replace him after 27 minutes. The match turned into a pretty intense forward battle, but as the game went on we slowly got on top, and with just a minute remaining I got the ball after an interception deep in our own half and sprinted for the line. The events of the last 24 hours almost caught up with me while I was running down the wing, but I just managed to make the line for the try. I remember thinking: 'I won't be doing this again.' But it was nice to sign the whole thing off with something a bit special, otherwise it would have been something of an anti-climax. And both of the teams I played for won, so at least I got double winning-pay.

I lot of people seemed to think that I'd get confused about which game I was playing when I was on the pitch. But that's nonsense: playing League one day and Union the next is as different as playing squash one day and tennis the next. Of course there are differences and you have to concentrate: in Rugby Union you've got to try to hold your position more because the game is much more structured, while in Rugby League you tend to follow the ball and support. I got through the games reasonably well, though, and didn't make any serious mistakes, but I was really tired and my overall contribution over both games wasn't that great.

The cameras seemed to follow me everywhere during the two days and there was a lot of press coverage about me over the weekend. Quite a few journalists – mainly those from the Union side – said things like 'Martin doesn't do himself any favours with this circus-type publicity stunt.' But it wasn't simply a publicity stunt, it was just that I was presented with a problem, and in a situation like that you can either whinge about it and just play one game – which might have been the sensible thing to do – or turn the whole thing around and try to make it into something positive.

I agree that things can backfire if a bit of a circus starts to develop. There's more pressure on you to perform, which makes it hard to concentrate, and all the media attention tends to gee up the opposition. But I didn't want Bedford to think that I didn't care, because the Rotherham game was an important league fixture for them. Some people didn't agree with what I did, but that's their problem. One article said: 'We see him neither of Union or League,' and I can see what the writer was getting at. The reactions of the different sets of supporters were interesting, too. In the game at Warrington the fans were saying: 'Eff off back to Rugby Union'; the Union spectators don't use as much profanity, but they still made their views known. They were telling me to go back to Rugby League or daytime TV – which I thought was quite funny.

After the game Gareth drove me down to Miss Moneypenny's, a club in Birmingham, where Lee, Mick and Dermot, who run the club, made me most welcome. On

Sunday Gareth took me back to London and drove back to Manchester the following day. All credit to Gareth, he really helped me out that weekend.

There was a certain amount of relief when my mad weekend was over, and I was very tired, both mentally and physically. I can't see anyone else repeating what I did – and I know I certainly won't be trying it again – but I had the satisfaction of doing something unique. Who knows, maybe in ten years time, on *A Question of Sport,* something will come up like: 'Which clubs did Martin Offiah play both Rugby League and Rugby Union for, in consecutive days in 1997?'

13
A New Beginning

I had some time on my hands during the summer, because the 1996/97 Union season was over and I'd played the last of my contracted games for the Broncos. So I started thinking about where I was in my life and where I wanted to be.

My outlook on life has changed as I've got older. Normally, people tend to be a bit wild and outrageous when they are young and calm down as they get older, but the reverse seems to be happening in my case. When I was growing up I was so focused on my rugby career that I was almost introverted. I wouldn't say that I was scared of trying things or of overstepping the mark, it's just that I didn't allow anything to deflect me from my aim of becoming successful at sport. I was only 21 when I went to Widnes, for example, and lived in a house on my own. It would have been easy for me to go off the rails, because there was nobody to tell me what to do or impose any rules. But I didn't drink, because I didn't compare myself to other rugby players. I looked at athletes and saw that they weren't out all the time getting drunk, so I thought I wouldn't either – because living like that might slow me up; besides, Ellery Hanley, with whom I spent a lot of time, didn't drink.

But as I got into my late twenties I began to think that I might be missing out, and that when I got older I might start to regret not doing so many things. When I was starting out all I wanted to do was to become the best rugby player that I possibly could, but when I started to feel that I'd achieved that goal I realised that there were other things that I wanted to do. I still loved scoring tries, and got the same buzz as always when I crossed the line, but I started to feel that I wanted more from my life. So I started to expand my horizons and went out a lot more.

My re-introduction to drink, after that bad experience when I was 15, had come on the Wigan team bus after we'd beaten Widnes at Wembley, in 1993. I felt I was old enough to handle it and I remember thinking: 'What the hell – if it kills me, it kills me. I'm going to be 30 soon, I could be dead.' I'd always believed that you have to sacrifice certain things to get what you want, and maybe I thought that I didn't need to sacrifice as much by then; I was old enough to handle it, too. I still don't consider myself a big drinker, but as I've grown older I've been able to enjoy myself more and still keep a grip on things. It's helped, too, because people have always been a bit suspicious of anybody who doesn't drink, and now the times when I've felt closest to my team-mates have been the ones when I've been totally blitzed. I think that the problem with a lot of sportsmen – George Best is an example – is that all the fame and fortune comes too early for them. But I kept myself in check until I was 26 or 27, and by that time I felt that I was mature enough to know what I had to do to stay at the top. Now I can go out on a Saturday and have a good time – but I'll be back on track come the Monday.

Once I thought that I would continue to be successful if I just kept everything in balance, so I tried to keep my weight constant and all my little rituals the same. I'd always been very superstitious, always making sure that I was in bed before midnight on the night before a game, for example. Once or twice I've got into bed just a minute or two after midnight and I've thought: 'Oh no.' I really believed that I wouldn't play well if I didn't stick to my routines. But now I'm trying to phase my superstitions out. My sweat bands will probably be the last of them to go, though. I leave them off now when I go out, but I still have to wear them when I'm playing. And I never have sex the night before a game, which has caused one or two problems with certain of my girlfriends. When you're playing twice a week and training, it can be difficult to maintain a relationship.

Slowly but surely, I've been changing. For example, a couple of years ago I realised that I'd had the same hairstyle for about ten years so I suddenly decided it was time for something new. So I got an electric razor and shaved all my hair off. The following day I walked into a bar in Manchester and a lot of people who had known me for a long time didn't recognise me – even my girlfriend's sister Charlotte didn't realise who I was at first. I must have been overdue for a change. Then I went to a party at the Hacienda Club and got completely smashed, and the next day there was a photograph of me with a girl on each arm in the *Manchester Evening News*. The caption read: 'Martin Offiah Shows off his New Hairstyle with two Friends' – so my new hairstyle was news. I was bald for a while, but keeping the style up became a bit of a pain, because every weekend I had to shave my head – then I decided to grow it a bit and dye it. It was blond during the summer of 1995, and when the season started I decided to keep it like that. For a little while I had the nickname 'Guinness', and the Wigan crowd used to call me 'pure genius'. But then we were due to play at St Helens, and there was no way that I was going to Knowsley Road with blond hair. I felt sure the Saints fans would have been working on their insults, so I thought I'd fool them and decided to change my hair colour to blue. And because Wigan were playing in their change strip of blue, everyone thought that I was dying my hair to go with the kit. Afterwards, I went through a phase of dying it in a variety of different colours.

All in all, I feel I've been reborn over the last couple of years. I had a long conversation with Shaun Edwards. We were in a club called 'Golden' (also known as 'The Void') in Stoke which is run by three mates of mine, Rocky, Dave and Briggsy. We talked about life and rugby. It certainly made a great impression on me, as did getting into the different world of club culture, where you meet people who have completely different backgrounds – both made me more open to different experiences. For example, I wouldn't have been seen dead in a gay club years ago, but now I don't think about it; in fact I now have friends who are gay. And my taste in music has changed, too. I used to be really rigid, in that I only liked soul music, but now I like all types of music and I'm a huge fan of Oasis.

I think that I really started to come out of my shell in 1995. My conversation with Shaun helped to change my outlook, and during the following few months I experienced highs and lows that convinced me that I should alter the way I looked at things. The low point came when Wigan lost to Wakefield Trinity at Central Park and I was booed by the crowd for my performance; and the high point came when I scored that fantastic length-of-the-field try against Leeds in the 1994 Challenge Cup Final. The contrast made me realise how fickle the game can be, and I began to treat rugby more as a job – though a job that I still enjoyed enormously. I still wanted to be successful and make a lot of money, but I realised that I wouldn't be playing the game forever. Up until then rugby had been my entire life and I'd cared so much about the game that it almost hurt.

I started going out with Shaun a lot and formed a really strong bond with him. But I didn't really get on with him when we first met, so it's ironic that our talk should have changed my life so much. I first came across him during my first season with Widnes, when we were both selected for a President's XIII. We played against each other a number of times after that, which was difficult because Shaun really hates his opponents. Then we roomed together, later in my first season, on the first leg of the 1988 Great Britain tour, which kicked off in Papua New Guinea. But that didn't work out either, because we were so different. Anyone who knows Shaun will tell you that he's got some really quirky habits: he likes to take a nap in the afternoon, for example; he loves sleeping with the window open; and he doesn't like putting the central heating on. I'd often go back to our room in the afternoon and find him asleep with the curtains drawn. He also likes to go to bed early, so if you dared to come back and put the television on all hell would break loose. I'm completely different, because I like to stay up late. One evening I came back and found him in bed asleep with the plug ripped off the television: he hadn't taken the easy option of simply pulling the plug out of the socket; instead he'd wrenched the flex out of the plug, leaving just bare wires. I know that there has to be give and take, but I also knew that the arrangement just wasn't going to work out – so I moved out and ended up sharing with Ellery Hanley.

Shaun and I were both friendly with Ellery, so we all used to go out together. We still had our differences, though. I remember getting into trouble with his dad once over something I'd said about him on television. It was when I was at Widnes and Wigan, as usual, were at Wembley, playing St Helens, and I was in the studio working for the BBC. Shaun made a big tackle and I said something along the lines of: 'A big hit from Shaun Edwards, who is not known as a big hitter, stopped him in his tracks.' I thought that was fair enough, because I wasn't being critical of him – far from it. But a few days later I got a letter from someone called 'Jackie Edwards', who I assumed was his mum, having a go at me for criticising Shaun. It really was quite a strong letter, and said that I would never be a good enough rugby player to lace his boots. Eventually I got to know Shaun, and realised that Jackie was his dad, but I still didn't have the nerve to ask him about it until, it came up one day, when I'd been at Wigan for more than a year. Shaun and I were sitting down and he suddenly turned round and said: 'What about that thing you said about me at Wembley?' I couldn't believe that he still remembered it, let alone that it still obviously rankled with him. However, I eventually got to know Shaun's dad and all his family quite well, and now I stay at their house if I'm ever up in Wigan.

A lot of people don't know how to take Shaun, because there are a lot of different sides to his character, and one of them is that he can be pretty abrupt. And while he's certainly had an influence on me, I think that I've also influenced him. He became much more flamboyant while we were both at Wigan and you see him doing things today that he never would have done a few years ago. And now that Shaun's with me at the Broncos, we still see a lot of each other.

One thing about Shaun in our Wigan days was that you could guarantee that any new player that came into the team would get a bollocking from him during a game sooner or later. Sometimes it was embarrassing, but you'd be given a real verbal lashing whoever you were. He had a go at Henry Paul once and carried on giving him grief for most of the game, but just before the end of the match an announcement came over the loudspeakers: 'And today's Man of the Match is Henry Paul.' I thought that was really funny. Shaun had been criticising him for most of the game and there he was being awarded Man of the Match!

I had my own technique with new players. When Simon Haughton and Kris Radlinski, two young players, came into the Wigan first team I decided to have a bit of fun. I used to take the mickey out of Simon, saying he couldn't pass, so I told him that his task for the season was to set me up for a try; then I told Kris that his mission was to give Shaun a bollocking during a televised game. I said, 'You've got to get right in his face and really have a go at him.' Simon Haughton did his job by giving me a scoring pass in the last game of the Centenary season against Leeds, but I don't think Kris ever managed his task.

I was also thinking about the whole business of Rugby League and Rugby Union during the summer. There have been major changes in both Rugby Union and Rugby League since I first played rugby, and I think that each code can learn things from the other one. Union has become professional, and I think it's trying to improve itself as a spectacle – I don't think that this was one of its priorities beforehand, but money has changed things. And I think that the sport would be a better spectacle if the game could be made to flow more. As with Rugby League, a lot of the improvements in Union are driven by the Southern Hemisphere: watching the Super-12 competition is like watching a different game – it's so much more exciting. Even though their teams' defences are meant to be great, so many points are scored because the game is played at such a fast pace, and as a result there are more gaps and more tries. I think a lot of this is down to the referees' interpretation of the laws: they like the game to flow, whereas in this country it's more stop-start, because the officials tend to blow up for the majority of infringements.

As far as the organisation of the game is concerned I think that most Union clubs have begun to realise that having a full-time professional squad is the way to go. And it's essential to have experts involved in all aspects of training, from fitness conditioners to weights specialists. In fact, I think it would have been hard for the Lions to beat South Africa in 1997 without the advent of professionalism. To begin with, they wouldn't have been able to call on the ex-league players, such as Alan Tait, John Bentley, Scott Gibbs, Scott Quinnell and Allan Bateman, who are not only great players but they've come from a professional environment. And because every member of the squad had been a professional for 12 months they were able to prepare properly and attain the level of fitness needed on such a tour. As a result, the Lions beat a side that would probably beat them eight times out of ten. But I have great respect for the way they performed, because although they didn't score a try in that crucial second Test they defended well and tackled hard, and their professionalism got them through.

Mind you, I think that League can also learn from Union. I think that Rugby League is too critical of itself, whereas in Union players and supporters seem to love the game in every shape or form – it seems to me a more unconditional love. If the whole world criticised the English game, I think that the Union supporters would rally round. By contrast, Rugby League followers are passionate about their sport but as soon as something goes wrong they are only too ready to criticise it.

And these general thoughts about the state of League and Union made me think during the summer about what I was going to do. I've talked about the problems I had at Bedford during the 1996/97 season: the personality clashes, the travelling, the fact that I didn't think that the Bedford set-up was fully professional, and so on. I hadn't been very happy at the club, and people had noticed it: on one occasion Rudi Straeuli, the South African forward, said that during the past he'd always seen me with a smile on my face when I was playing, but he'd only seen it on one or two occasions at Bedford. And I had to face the prospect of another season in Second Division rugby.

I'd also come to realise that it was Frank Warren, and his Sports Network company, rather than Paul Turner or Geoff Cooke, who had been responsible for me joining Bedford. There had been bit of friction with Paul and Geoff during the season, though I started to get on well with Paul and respect him, and I think that both of them thought that I wasn't really on board. I gather that Geoff Cooke had expressed some doubts about my commitment to the club and said that if I wasn't fully committed I wouldn't figure in his future plans – though I didn't really know what that meant.

I suppose that towards the end of the season I'd made it a bit obvious that I didn't really want to go back, but I was hoping that things would just sort themselves out, and I think that it became a question of who was going to get out of the situation first. The fact that we were playing in the Second Division hadn't helped, but the main problem for me was that the set-up was only semi-professional. I've been a professional for years, and what I love is just turning up and training when everything else has been taken care of. I don't think that the Union environment – with the shirt, blazer and tie bit – was for me. I'm not so concerned about the money, I just want to do something that I enjoy and get up every morning with a smile on my face. But the thought of getting up and going to Bedford to train was something that was beginning to make me feel physically sick. It wasn't because of any individual, but more due to the whole set-up. The thought of playing at Bedford for the next three years was just too much.

Anyway, Geoff Cooke asked to see me during the summer, and Alan McColm went along to see him. I still had three years to run on a contract that was very lucrative, but both sides agreed that a parting of the ways was the right thing to happen, and Alan eventually reached an agreement with the club. I was sent a letter saying that my contract with Bedford would be terminated on 31 August 1997.

Then I had a meeting with Harlequins coach Andy Keast about the possibility of playing Union at The Stoop. It was a couple of days before the deadline for registration of players for the European Cup, and the idea was that I'd sign the registration form and then sign a short-term deal; we'd discuss a longer contract later. I liked Andy, but I didn't want to be in the same situation as at Bedford, where one person wanted me at the club but perhaps not everyone connected with the club did. I thought, 'Martin, are you really ready to take another gamble?' And I asked myself what I really wanted out of the game. I didn't want to be someone who went from club to club just making as much money as he could. So I told Alan: 'Thank them for their offer but it's not what I really want to do.'

I heard that Andy Keast had spoken to Geoff Cooke about me – I don't know whether it was about the possibility that a transfer fee might be payable for me, or whatever – but I gather that Cooke didn't give me a very glowing report. I thought that was a bit unfair, and it left something of a nasty taste in the mouth. But Harlequins were still interested, despite whatever he said. I think one of the problems was that Cooke, who isn't the greatest man-manager, never really came to talk to me about things. I think he misunderstood me: maybe he just saw someone who was making too much money and driving a flash car. I always try and see things from other people's perspective, but I suppose it was a personality clash.

Anyway, I'm out of it now. And though I've lost out on a lucrative contract, I think I've gained in more ways than one. I agreed a deal with the Broncos until the end of the season and for another two years, playing for them full-time. I'm happy to concentrate on playing Rugby League, and I only need another nine tries to move up to number three on the all-time list of top try-scorers, behind Brian Bevan and Billy Boston. That'll be enough for me – if I'd continued to play Union and got injured, and lost the opportunity to score those nine tries I'd have felt bad, even though I could have earned a lot more money by carrying on in Union. And being involved with the Broncos again means that I'm at a club where there are people with real aspirations and ambitions. I also know that I'm really wanted there, because I checked with Tony Rea, the Chief Executive, as well as Maurice Lindsay and the people at Virgin.

Another reason for giving up Union was that I couldn't see myself playing rugby for almost 12 months a year any longer. I'd been thinking about what I was going to do when I retired from the game. I realised a long time ago that I'd never make a coach: at Wigan the younger players often used to ask the senior players for advice about the game, but the only time they came to me was when they were re-negotiating a new contract or they wanted to know how to get clubs in for free. So I certainly wasn't going to have a non-playing career in rugby. On the other hand, I knew that I'd be reasonably secure in a financial sense: ever since the early days, I've taken Dougie's advice and invested a large part of my earnings.

But what really interests me is seeing whether I can make a go of a career in the media and in acting. I know a few actors, and I've decided that when I finish playing I'm going to take up acting seriously. I thought of taking acting lessons one day a week when I came back to London, but my rugby schedule only gives me one day a week off, and I really have to rest on it. But when I retire I'll probably take a year off to study acting properly. I know it won't be easy but it's something I want to do – and as I've achieved success once in my life there's no reason why I can't be successful in something else.

In fact, I've already done some acting. I used to have a regular column in the *Sun*, and once I mentioned that I liked acting – I happened to say that the soap opera *Emmerdale* was particularly popular at Wigan. The piece was given the headline 'Martin for *Emmerdale*', and I think that someone must have talked about it at one of the show's script meetings because it turned out that one of the writers was a big Rugby League fan. At any rate, I was asked whether I'd like to appear on the show, and I agreed like a shot – though it was quite daunting when I got the script and had to start learning my lines! The scenes took two days to shoot and I really enjoyed the whole experience.

The storyline was that Terry, the barman at The Woolpack, was putting a Rugby League team together, and I was supposed to be his secret weapon. At first, it felt like the first day at a new school when I turned up on the set. Then someone said: 'Let's run through the scene that you're in, Martin.' So we did, and I think they were quite surprised that I knew my lines because Ian Botham had been on a previous programme and he hadn't learned his lines at all. But they seemed quite happy with what I was doing, and everyone who saw the episode was pleasantly surprised by how it went. Gary Connolly came along with me and was in some of the scenes, but the one line of dialogue he was given ended up on the cutting room floor. The story was that the team was a man short and someone turned to Gary and said: 'Do you fancy a game, mate?' He was meant to turn round and say 'Who, me?', but he couldn't do it properly so they cut the line. Gary wasn't bothered, though – he was more interested in the fact that they had real beer in The Woolpack! I thought that the whole thing was a really good laugh, but I couldn't talk about it too much, because Shaun Edwards was upset that he hadn't been invited!

The same scriptwriter also works on *Hollyoaks* and *Brookside*, and said that there might be a possibility of some more work, although I'd have to play myself again – I wasn't too happy about that, but beggars can't be choosers. So I played the boyfriend of one of the girls in *Hollyoaks*, and everyone there seemed to think things went well. If I was absolutely terrible I just wouldn't do it, but because people were complimentary it gave me some encouragement. But my appearance didn't go down too well with Tracy Shaw and Angela Griffin, a couple of friends of mine who play the hairdressers Maxine and Fiona in *Coronation Street*. They sent me a note calling me a traitor!

I think my love of performing stems from my mum and dad: my parents used to love musicals like *The Sound of Music*, *Seven Brides for Seven Brothers* and *West Side Story*, and when I was younger I used to learn all the songs from them. Television is the medium for me, and I've always said that I wanted to work in television after I retire. I've had lots of experience in front of the camera – from working at Wembley for the BBC when a big match is on to doing chat shows and game shows – but I want to get away from sport. I'm sure I could become a presenter for Sky Sports, but that's not what I want to do: I wouldn't like to be the Alan Hansen of Rugby League. I've done some modelling as well, though it's not a major earner for me; but it's a good way of building up your profile and getting yourself known. I've had a lot of spin-offs from the work I've done and I'm still with the CSI agency, which is based in London and caters mainly for sportsmen.

Apart from acting, I've dabbled with a few ventures, but I'm not the kind of person to put money into something in which I don't have any real interest. But one type of business that I might get involved with is club promotions. I enjoy clubbing, and over the years I've got to know a lot of the top DJs and club promoters up and down the country. My favourite club is Miss Moneypenny's in Birmingham, where I'm well looked after. Some people even say it's my second home. I'm particularly friendly with Cath Mackenzie, who books DJs for a lot of the top clubs. I know many of them personally, like my old school friend Mark Moore and the king himself, Allister Whitehead. I've always been into music, but when I first went to Widnes I hardly went out – and there wasn't much in the way of nightlife there anyway. But in 1991 I met a guy called Mark Worrall, who I used to see in a club called 'Mr Smith's', in Warrington. I never really liked him at the time: he used to wear jeans with big belts that would come up to his armpits, he had long hair, and he used to walk around the place as though he owned it.

Later we started talking and he told me that his two sisters had got into a fight in a pub over me because someone had been slagging me off. It turned out that he lived just a few miles from me and I started going out to clubs with him. I was going through a bad patch at the time – I'd just come back from playing for St George in Australia and was in dispute with Widnes, so I wasn't playing – and I really didn't want to stay in, because I'd just have brooded about what was going on, so I used to go out all the time with Mark. He really knew how to enjoy himself and I started going to more rave-type clubs with him. He knew a lot of people, too – DJs and the like – and it was Mark who introduced me to M People; I introduced him to

Ellery and Shaun, and he became great friends with them as well. Now I'm pretty well-known in clubland and clubs have become quite big business over the last few years, so running a club is something I'm thinking about doing when I retire.

I'm contracted for two more seasons with the London Broncos, and I haven't actually set a date for when I'll retire. As you get older, though, you realise that you're not immortal and you won't play forever. And I don't like getting sentimental about the game, though I must admit that I was a little sad when I saw Wigan doing so badly at the start of the 1997 season. When they lost to a weakened Bradford side and to Salford, I couldn't help thinking back to the days when we would have smashed both those sides by 70 points. Sometimes I put on old videos of Wigan matches and reminisce. I know that's silly, because I always told myself that I would never look back, but my time at Wigan was special. So many great things happened there, and I can't help remembering fondly some of the great days.

I don't see an image of myself hanging up my boots and walking out of the dressing room as if it was in the last few minutes of a Hollywood movie. It'll be more a matter of going off to do something else. I don't want to get to the stage where I don't want to play any more and find myself thinking: 'What am I going to do now?' Even so, I know that everything I have in life has come directly or indirectly from rugby, and all the various doors have opened for me because I've been successful in rugby: so wherever I am and whatever I do I'll always be a rugby player. I know that some time in the future I'll be with a group of people who may not know my background and when we watch a tough, high-contact game of Rugby League I'll be proud of the fact that I can say: 'I used to play that game when I was younger.' The one thing about being a winger and scoring lots of great tries is that somehow it makes you immortal. You know that they'll always be shown on television, in the same way that they show the tries of Billy Boston and Tom Van Vollenhoven, and it's a good feeling.

I see my retirement from rugby in a positive rather than a negative light, and when I stop playing I'll still believe that the day afterwards I can still go out and score a hat-trick. There will be a bit of a tear in my eye, but the decision will be one that I've made and not one that has been made for me. A lot of players have gone on too long and I don't want to be one of them. If I get to a stage in which I'm not really enjoying my rugby then I'll pack it in – as I have with Bedford. I realised pretty early on in my League career that I wouldn't stay in the game: I was never really into the rugby environment, and many of my friends didn't play, so I soon came to the conclusion that when I retired I wouldn't want to be one of those ex-pros who bang on about how things were better in their day. I'll have complete respect for the players who come after me.

The fact that I'm not married and don't have a family is partly because of the demands of my career. I'm pretty selfish with my time and what I do, and although I've had the support of my family I've always been a bit of an individual. But now I'm starting to enjoy myself and do the things that I denied myself when I was younger. For example, I had never been on holiday until 1995, and earlier in my career I would never have contemplated taking time off from rugby for a holiday. I feel as though I'm winding down a little bit in some ways – but I still look forward to playing. I see myself having kids in the future because I love children, and the only way I would ever be involved in the game after I've retired would be to coach youngsters.

I plan to go a bit mad when I eventually retire. I don't mean that I'll go completely off the rails, but I'll certainly live a little – at least for the first six months. I see it as a prize, some kind of a reward for all the time and effort I've put in over the years. Because even though playing rugby for a living is enjoyable, it's still hard work and I've had to deny myself things. And when I get through my mad stage I hope that I'll become a model citizen.

I went to Ibiza for a week after I'd made the decision to finish with Bedford and commit myself to the Broncos. The idea was to forget about everything, but even in Ibiza people came up to me and asked me what was happening – the hotel televisions carry Sky Sports and there's always someone watching the games. I was sitting outside one bar when a Spanish waiter came up and asked for my autograph, saying: 'I love that game.' But I was glad to get back to London, because I'd been looking forward to playing for the Broncos in the last Super League fixture of the season against the champions Bradford Bulls, on 31 August. After all the uncertainties of the past few months, it felt as if I was back where I belonged. And it was important that we won, because there was the Premiership to look forward to.

We won the game, by 28–24, and I scored two tries, including the winning one in the last few minutes. But to be honest that didn't really seem to be important ... it was the day that Diana, Princess of Wales, was killed tragically in a road accident in Paris. I'll remember that day for the rest of my life.

Career Statistics

Career Highlights

1965: Born 29 December in Hackney, north London, the third child of Nigerian parents who came to Britain to study. Brother Chike is three years older and sister Nina is one year older.

1972: Attends Thornhill primary school in Islington and dreams of being a striker for Arsenal.

1977: Follows elder brother Chike to Woolverstone Hall, an ILEA boarding school in Suffolk where they play rugby, not football. Scores his first tries in a rugby-type game called 'Stonehenge' which involves all the first-year boys.

1980: Gives up fencing to concentrate on rugby and decides he's going to play for England.

1983: Plays senior rugby for Ipswich RUFC while still at school and is subsequently selected for Eastern Counties.

1985: Leaves school and spends the summer on the ground-staff at Essex but one game for the Second XI convinces him that his future does not lie in cricket. Joins Rosslyn

Park RUFC and makes his first team debut on Tuesday, 19 November against Loughborough Colleges.

1986: Ends his first season in senior rugby as the club's top try scorer with 13. Begins the new season in sparkling form, and a burgeoning reputation as a spectacular try scorer sees Martin selected for London Division to play the North. Although well beaten, he manages to score London's only try.

1987: A successful second season for Rosslyn Park ends with him as top try scorer and having furthered his reputation with the Penguins in the Hong Kong Sevens and the Barbarians. Represents England Students in France but in June turns professional with Widnes and make his debut against Halifax. He doesn't score until his third game against Runcorn in the Lancashire Cup but then goes on to score in the next 15.

1988: Collects a hat-trick against St Helens on Easter Monday to help Widnes clinch the Championship, their first for 10 years. A few weeks later Widnes beat St Helens in the Premiership Final at Old Trafford 38–14 and Martin finishes the season as the league's top try scorer with 44. Wins the Man of Steel award and is selected for the Great Britain tour of Australasia. Scores a try in the memorable 26–12 win over Australia in the Third Test in Sydney, Great Britain's first for 10 years.

1989: Scores a hat-trick against Wigan in the final league game of the season to enable Widnes to retain the First Division Championship trophy. A try in the Premiership Final against Hull also helps Widnes to an 18–10 victory and Martin ends the season again as the league's top try scorer with 60. Spends the summer playing for Eastern Suburbs in Australia. In October scores two tries as Widnes memorably defeat the Canberra Raiders 30–18 at Old Trafford to take the World Club Championship.

1990: The rest of the season proves a disappointment but Widnes once again win the Premiership Trophy beating Bradford Northern 28–6 in the final. Martin ends the season as the league's top try scorer with 45 for the third year in succession. Tours New Zealand and Papua New Guinea with Great Britain and begins the new domestic season by scoring a try in Widnes 24–8 win over Wigan in the Charity Shield at Swansea. At Castleford on 6 October he breaks the record for the fastest century of Division One tries.

1991: Scores a record breaking five tries for Great Britain against France at Headingley in February. However, he becomes disillusioned with Widnes, the club having failed to get to the Challenge Cup final again. Scores his last try for Widnes as they lose to Hull 14–4 in the Premiership at Old Trafford but still ends the season as top try scorer with 49. Spends the summer with the St George club in Sydney and returns to Widnes in September but refuses to play for them and asks for a transfer.

1992: Signs for Wigan for the world record fee of £440,000 and makes his debut on 5 January against Wakefield Trinity but fails to score. A month later helps Wigan win the Nissan World Sevens in Sydney with 11 tries in five matches. Collects five touchdowns in Wigan's 71–10 demolition of Bradford Northern in the Challenge Cup semi-final and goes on to help Wigan win the First Division Championship. Wins his first Challenge Cup final medal when Wigan beat Castleford 28–12 scoring two tries and collecting the Lance Todd Trophy as man of the match. Two weeks later runs in an amazing 10 tries as Wigan humiliate Leeds 74–6 in the semi-final of the Premiership. and scores two more in the 48–16 win over St Helens in the final. In August he is fined £250 for failing to collect his losers medal after Wigan are beaten 17–0 by St Helens at Gateshead in the Charity Shield. Martin is featured in a huge poster campaign on the London Underground, 'Will the Aussies Catch Offiah at Wembley?' to promote the World Cup final but Great Britain are beaten 10-6 and a week later Wigan lose 22–8 to the Brisbane Broncos at Central Park in the World Club Challenge.

1993: Martin is dropped by Great Britain for the match against France at Headingley because of doubts over his fitness. Wigan retain the First Division title and Martin collects his second Challenge Cup winners medal as Wigan beat his old club Widnes 20–14 but the occasion is marred when former team-mate Richie Eyres is sent off for a high tackle on him. Ends the season with 38 tries and jets off to play for Eastern Suburbs but sustains a serious shoulder injury in his first match and returns home needing major surgery, subsequently missing the first two months of the domestic season.

1994: After a difficult first half to the season everything works out well as Martin helps Wigan to another Championship and scores two tries in their Wembley triumph over Leeds to collect the Lance Todd Trophy for the second time. Wigan also beat Castleford in the Premiership final and then become the only British side to win the World Club Challenge away from home when they beat the Brisbane Broncos 20–14 in Queensland.

1995: Becomes leading try scorer for the first time since leaving Widnes, notching up 53. In October, helps England beat Australia in opening game of Centenary World Cup at Wembley but lose to them in the final 16–8. Out jumps Jonathan Edwards on BBC's Sports Personality of the Year Award.

1996: Helps Wigan win the Centenary Championship, Rugby League's last as a winter sport, and the Regal Trophy. Martin is one of the stars of Wigan's triumph in the Middlesex Sevens but in August leaves the club to play league for the London Broncos and union for Bedford in a joint transfer deal believed to be worth £300,000. Appears on television soaps *Emmerdale* and *Hollyoaks*.

1997: Awarded the MBE in the Queen's New Year's Honours List, plays Rugby League for the Broncos and Rugby Union for Bedford on consecutive days in March. Finishes the season at Bedford with 13 tries, collects a hat-trick in the Broncos's 28–10 victory over Paris St Germain on Good Friday, the fiftieth of his career. In July is awarded an honorary degree from John Moores University in Liverpool and the following month turns his back on Rugby Union by terminating his contract with Bedford and negotiating a new full-time deal with the London Broncos.

Professional Career Facts and Figures (as at end of August 1997)

- Signed by Widnes from Rosslyn Park RU
- Widnes debut v Halifax (h), 30 August 1987
- Transferred to Wigan for a still world record cash deal of £440,000
- Wigan debut v Wakefield Trinity (h), 5 January 1992
- Transferred to London Broncos in August 1996. This was a joint transfer as Offiah also signed for Bedford RU. The total figure believed to be £300,000 with Bedford paying the larger amount.
- London Broncos debut v Warrington (h), 4 August 1996
- Bedford debut v Rotherham (h), 19 October, 1997

Records
Widnes
- Most tries in a season: 58 in 1988/89 (he had broken the old record with 42 the previous season – his first in Rugby League)
- Most tries in a match: 5 v Warrington (h), 15 March 1989 (joint record)

Wigan
- Most tries in a match: 10 v Leeds (h), 10 May 1992 (joint record)

Great Britain
- Most tries in a match: 5 v France at Leeds, 16 February 1991

England
- Most tries in a match: 4 v France at Gateshead, 12 June 1996 (joint record)

Other records

- Has been rugby league's top try scorer six times
- Raced to the fastest career century of Division One* tries in 70 matches. No other player has reached the milestone in fewer than 100 matches
- Twice equalled the Division One* record of scoring at least one try in 11 successive matches as follows
  Widnes 1987/88: 1–1–1–1–2–1–2–2–2–1–2
  Wigan 1995/96: 1–1–1–2–1–1–1–1–1–1–5
- Most Premiership finals: 8 (Widnes 1988, 89, 90, 91 and Wigan 1992, 93, 94, 95)
- Most Premiership final wins: 6 (Widnes 1988, 89, 90 and Wigan 1992, 94, 95)

Other notable feats (not records)

- Sixth in all-time try scorers chart with 438 tries (all matches)
- Second in all-time Division One/Super League try scorers chart with 248 tries
- Scored 50 hat-tricks including 10 tries (once), five (six times), four (12 times), three (31 times)
- Great Britain Test rankings: 26 tries (third); 104 points (9th); 33 appearances (5th)

Cup Finals and Championships

- Challenge Cup final appearances at Wembley: 1992 (2t), 1993, 1994 (2t), 1995. All with Wigan and a winner each time

* Refers to the old Division One championship and the 1995/96 Centenary Championship

- Lance Todd Trophy winner: Wigan v Castleford 1992, Wigan v Leeds 1994
- Championship winners medals
- Widnes 1987/88, 1988/89; Wigan 1991/92, 1992/93, 1993/94, 1994/95, 1995/96
- Regal Trophy finals: Widnes 1989 (L); Wigan 1993 (W), 1994 (L), 1995 (W, 1t), 1996 (W)
- World Club Challenge: Widnes 1989 (W, 2t); Wigan 1992 (L); 1994 Wigan (W)
- Lancashire Cup finals: Widnes 1990 (W,1t); Wigan 1992 (W)
- Charity Shield: Widnes 1988 (W,1t), 1989 (W, 1t), 1990 (W, 1t); Wigan 1992 (L)
- Premiership – (see Records)

Offiah's season by season try scoring figures

	App	*Tries*	*Position*
Widnes			
1987/88	35	42+1t GB and 1t RLXIII	1st
1988/89	41	58+2t GB(inc 1t non-Test)	1st
1989/90	32	40+5t GB	1st
1990/91	37	41+8t GB	1st
Wigan			
1991/92	15+1(r)	30	7th
1992/93	38	30+2t England	5th
1993/94	34	35+2t GB	3rd
1994/95	38	53	1st
1995/96	23	26+2t England	1st
1996	10	12+4t England	–

London Broncos

1996	4	3
1997	14	13 (to end of August 97)

Totals

Widnes	145	181
Wigan	158 +1(r)	186
London B	18	16
GB	34*	27*
1988 tour	7+2(r)	17 (Not inc 2t in 4 Tests)
1990 tour	1	0 (Not inc 2t in 3 Tests)
1992 tour	1	2 (Not inc 5t in 6 Tests)
England	5	8
RL XIII	1	1
Lancashire	1	0

	App	Tries
Grand total	271+3(r)	438

Also kicked one conversion and three drop goals for Wigan and one drop goal for England

Offiah is currently sixth in the all time try scoring list

Brian Bevan	796
Billy Boston	571
Alf Ellaby	446
Eric Batten	443
Lionel Cooper	441
Martin Offiah	438

* Includes one appearance and a try in a non-Test match

Offiah has also played club rugby in Australia as follows:

	App	Tries
Eastern Suburbs		
1989	12	9
1993	1	0
St George		
1991	14	11
Totals	27	20

Rugby Union

	App	Tries
Bedford		
1996/97	21+1(r)	13

Index